IN THIS

DOROTHY McRAE-McMAHON
Church in Australia. For ten years sh.
Street Uniting Church in the centre ᵥ   ᵤr five
years the National Director for Missioᵢ   ᵤₙ. She was a
member of the World Council of Chuᵢ   .ᵥorship Committee
for its Canberra Assembly and Moderator of its Worship Committee for the Harare Assembly. Her community awards indicate
her interests and concerns. She has received a Jubilee Medal from
the Queen for work with women in NSW (1977), an Australian
Government Peace Award (1986), the Australian Human Rights
Medal (1988) and an Honorary Doctorate of Letters from
Macquarrie University in Sydney for her work with minorities
and her contribution to the spiritual life of the community (1992).

Also by the author:

Being Clergy, Staying Human
(Alban Institute, Washington, Australia 1992)

Echoes of Our Journey: Liturgies of the People
(Joint Board of Christian Education, Melbourne 1993)

The Glory of Blood, Sweat and Tears:
Liturgies for Living and Dying
(Joint Board of Christian Education, Melbourne 1996)

Everyday Passions: A Conversation on Living
(ABC Books, Sydney 1998)

Liturgies for the Journey of Life
(SPCK 2000)

Prayers for Life's Particular Moments
(SPCK 2001)

Daring Leadership in the 21st Century
(ABC Books, Sydney 2001)

In This Hour

Liturgies for Pausing

Dorothy McRae-McMahon

Published in Great Britain in 2001
Society for Promoting Christian Knowledge
Holy Trinity Church
Marylebone Road
London NW1 4DU

British Library Cataloguing-in-Publication Data

A catalogue record for this book is available from the British Library

ISBN 0–281–05444–4

Typeset by Wilmaset Ltd, Birkenhead, Wirral
Printed in Great Britain by
The Cromwell Press, Trowbridge, Wiltshire

Contents

Introduction

All worship is a pausing in our life, or at least a different style of ongoing in our journey. In worship we stop our usual way of working, playing or struggling on our own and come into another environment for our living. In traditional worship there is usually a familiar framework for doing this. Perhaps because we know it well, we can live within its structures of prayer, music and Eucharist, its concentration on the foundations of faith in ways of our choosing – in silences, in creative emptiness or in a focus of our choosing, placing ourselves in its creative possibilities for encounter with our God.

In contemporary contextual worship, the same can happen. However, sometimes, precisely because it is contextual, contemporary worship can invite a stronger corporate focus on some particular aspect of the faith journey. This can be a scriptural focus which brings Word and worship more tightly together, or it can be a focus on some aspect of community life. The foundations of the faith still lie firmly underneath the best contemporary worship, but there is sometimes a greater freedom to focus more sharply on some aspect of the faith.

As the church offers its liturgical skills to the wider community, it invites the community to pause in its rushing life and focus too on some aspect of its life. In this it models the honouring, the taking seriously of the human journey, the marking of its significant life in grieving and celebration.

The liturgies in this book have been formed during my ministry with people who were prepared to come together for a special hour. They were people in congregations, in church councils, gathered in a home or for a special time when people draw apart with supportive friends for remembering and healing. They invite you to take from their ideas, their experiences of preparing that hour, something which may make your hour mean more to you.

In this hour, we pause. In this hour we give to ourselves an opportunity to meet our God and meet each other in ways which may go beyond anything we could have imagined. We can never put a boundary on the possibilities for the bringing in of a new 'order', a new perspective, a new energy, a new dream which may be ours in this hour. In this hour, we pray.

Dorothy McRae-McMahon

Using these Liturgies

Obviously pastors who use these liturgies will take account of their own context and the way their people use liturgical material, just as I did in bringing these prayers together.

Most of these liturgies would benefit by the inclusion of music. I have left it for the users to decide what music they will add and at what point. Music is a very cultural thing, even in the church these days. There are now very few 'well-known hymns' and sung responses!

At the beginning of each liturgy I have noted the main resources needed for symbolic images or acts already written into the liturgy. I always assume that people add their own ideas about preparing the environment for liturgical events – that they will bring in their own cloths, candles, crosses, banners, contextual images or symbols, or anything else that might enhance the moment, or that they may choose to simply use the prayers.

When a liturgy has been specifically prepared around certain Bible readings, those readings are included, otherwise it is assumed that people will select their own as appropriate. Having said that, some of the services which are attached to certain readings may well be used in other contexts and with other readings.

The concept of a book of liturgy is that it will give ideas to people, and that they will adapt prayers and symbols for their own context. Good contemporary liturgy is an evolving event, made in spirit and in truth for each people and each place.

In This Hour, Let us Celebrate

God is with us, this we believe.
For we have seen the signs of grace
in every place, in every generation.

The beauty of the creation,
in all its pristine wonder,
is not the only dwelling place of the Creator.

This, our God, is born again in cities as well as stables,
is found in holy places
in the modern market place
and sits with us in coffee shops
and by the one who hopefully sings a song
on the streets of this day.

The Spirit dances on concrete
and holds in comfort
those who walk with briefcases and shopping bags.
The God who is more than we can ever name or know
is beside us in every work place
and every hidden home of our body, mind and soul.

THERE YOU WERE
A celebration of the city

For this service you will need

- *Pictures or posters or other symbols of the city in which you live*
- *A cloth to image a pathway through the city, placed from a cross on the table and spread down towards the centre of the people*
- *Lengths of bright ribbon in a basket for placing on the cloth*

OPENING SENTENCES

We lifted our eyes to the hills
and they seemed very distant
in their mystery and grace.
We thought of still waters and lakes with calm and storms
as we walked by tall buildings on hard pavements.
And then, there you were among the publicans
and the crowds who stood on street corners in the city.
There you were,
watching us with tender love among our milling life,
the God who is with us in each place.

CONFESSION

Sometimes it is easier to imagine you staying far away from us,
    O God.
We hold to a hope that, if you are in the distance,
you cannot address our lives so directly.
But then, a distant God might not understand
the complexities with which we struggle,
and that feels lonely and we become anxious
that you will not forgive us.

Silent reflection

So, here we are, in our humanness, O God,
with all its messiness and pretences.

If we tend to hold you
in some romantic green and glorious place:
Forgive our limiting your presence among us.

If we are tempted to push you away from us:
Forgive our lack of faith in your love.

When we think you do not see us:
**Be present on the road before us
and remind us of our calling again, Jesus Christ.**

For we are not the people we would want to be
as we stand before your holiness and grace.
Amen.

ASSURANCE

Jesus said, 'I will send you a comforter' who will never leave you.
There is no place which is distant from the love of God.
There is no person at whose table God will not sit.
We are forgiven!
Thanks be to God.

READINGS

SERMON/REFLECTION

AFFIRMATION

In response to the word, let us affirm our faith together:

**God is with us, this we believe.
For we have seen the signs of grace
in every place, in every generation.**

**The beauty of the creation,
in all its pristine wonder,
is not the only dwelling place of the Creator.**

**This, our God, is born again in cities as well as stables,
is found in holy places
in the modern market place
and sits with us in coffee shops
and by the one who hopefully sings a song
on the streets of this day.**

The Spirit dances on concrete
and holds in comfort
those who walk with briefcases and shopping bags.
The God who is more than we can ever name or know
is beside us in every work place
and every hidden home of our body, mind and soul.

OFFERING

INTERCESSION

Today we remember those who find God crowded out
of their lives in the city,
those who are swallowed up by its overwhelming life,
or left behind in the rush,
those who are painfully alone in the centre of many people
and the ones who cannot find the source of life
in its seemingly barren pathways.

Silent prayer

We pray for all your people and the fragile life of the city:
**Give to us eyes to see you here, O God,
ears to hear your voice among the many sounds
and hearts which love this place as you do.**

We pray this in the name of the one who enters every place.
Amen.

CELEBRATION OF THE CITY

Let us celebrate that God is here in the city!
For we have seen God here.
We will name those times and places
and mark the way of the Christ with bright ribbons.

*The people remember places, people and moments when they have seen
God in the city and place ribbons along the cloth pathway*

Hallelujah! Hallelujah!
God is with us!

A hallelujah is sung or a doxology

DISMISSAL AND BLESSING

Go forth into the city.
Go in peace and faith.
And may your hand be in the hand of Christ,
your feet follow the God of all history
and your heart be lifted up by the joyful Spirit of God.
Amen.

∽

CELEBRATE THE UNITY OF HUMANKIND
A celebration of multicultural society

This ritual can be helpful in communities which are suffering from racism and prejudice. It can be a service of the church with prayers and religious references, a multifaith service with prayers from various traditions, or, as here, simply an initiative by the church which offers an open community ritual for all people. The ideas for this service come from one held in the Pitt Street Uniting Church in the centre of Sydney, Australia.

Preparation

Several leading citizens can be asked to tell a story of human unity. In Sydney, the three story-tellers were a leading High Court judge, a popular television presenter and a Jewish woman. People from several different ethnic backgrounds can be invited to come forward and offer their ethnicity into the community, maybe bringing with them some symbol of their culture.

The addition of music and singing will enhance the ritual greatly – local songs or tunes which are added, not just at the points noted, but sung as refrains through the receiving of gifts.

For this ritual you will need

- *A large candle*
- *A long purple cloth*
- *A very long gold cloth*
- *Several pairs of scissors*
- *A large table for the placing of symbols or a space in the centre of the people*

OPENING

The unity of humankind is a possible miracle
lying in the universe waiting to be realized,
as part of its interweaving harmonies,
its colours blending into beauty and shining light.

A large candle is lit

The unity of humankind is a gracious choice,
born of respect and dignity for all,
carried forward in the wonder of discovering new things in each
    other
and bonded together in deep and costly acceptance.

A purple cloth is swathed around the candle

The unity of humankind is a dream of hope,
a determination of the human spirit
as it connects with a larger good,
and forms a circle of wholeness.

*A gold cloth is placed in a circle around the purple cloth, leaving a
circular space in between for the placing of ethnic symbols*

MUSIC OR SINGING

GRIEVING

We do not yet live in a miracle.
We have not yet brought in the dream for humankind.
We grieve this.
We grieve for the suffering of the excluded,
the unrecognized, the vilified, the hated,
and those who feel alone among us.
Sadness fills our hearts as we think of this pain.

A silence is kept

In brief words, let us say aloud our longings as we feel this
    sadness.
What people and situations come into our minds as concerns?

The people share their longings

In sharing these longings we give power to the forces of love
  among us.
Let us stand firm in hope.

STORIES OF HUMAN UNITY
Told by community leaders as personal stories

THE OFFERING
In our community lie great gifts
which come from our differing histories and cultures.
I now invite some people to come forward and offer their
  ethnicity,
with all that this carries,
into the life of our community.
When they bring forward a symbol of their ethnic life,
they will tell us what it is and place it within the golden cloth,
and say:
I offer my *(ethnicity e.g. Greek life, Indian life)* into this community.
I invite you to respond:
And we gladly receive it!

The people come forward

And now, is there anyone else who would like to offer their ethnic
  gifts into this community?
If so, please stand or come forward and make your offering to us.

Other people may come forward

SINGING

BONDING AND SENDING OUT
We are each a part of this.
I invite you to come and cut a piece of the gold cloth
which is the symbol of your place in the creation of the circle of
  community.

The people come forward and do so

I invite you now to gather in a circle.

The people gather in a circle, or they place a hand on the shoulder of the person next to them if that is more practical

Here we have heard and seen a great possibility
which already lies in our community,
one which could be a living creation
of the unity of humankind.
Together we could make it real!
Will we do this together?
Yes we will!

Will we lift the hopes of this our community?
Yes, we will!

Go then, in courage and peace
to be a new day and a new world.
So be it!

MUSIC OR SINGING

It is good to have a party afterwards

↤

CELEBRATION OF A CHILD

The leader for this little ritual could be a minister, family member or friend, or the role could be alternated between the parents. Sometimes people do not choose to have their child baptized or wish to delay that, but would like to celebrate their child and make a commitment to them. This ritual can be either religious or without religious language.

For this ritual you will need

- *Three candles and two tapers*
- *A bowl of earth*
- *Those present need to be invited ahead of time to bring something for the 'time capsule' – a message, gift or symbol which they would like the child to have at 14 years old*
- *The 'time capsule' – a suitable box or bag or other container*

OPENING

This is a moment of pausing.
It is a chosen moment, after *(one month/one year, etc.)* in the life of
    (Name).
In this moment we will celebrate *her/his* life among us,
we will commit ourselves to *her/his* love and care
and we will offer *(Name)* our blessing for *her/his* life's journey.
This is a rite of passage for *her/him* and for us, *her/his* family and
    friends,
a moment of significance.

REMEMBERING

One month/One year ago *(state time)*, *(Name)* was born
and our life changed
in the light of *her/his* presence among us.

A candle is lit

In this child, we have received many things:

Parents name these things first and then others follow

All these things, and more, we have already received from this
    child.
**We celebrate all the gifts which *she/he* brings to us in *her/his*
    life.**

The child is lifted up

COMMITMENT

From the day *she/he* was born we have loved *her/him*
and we will go on in this love and care.

Each parent lights a candle and places it alongside the child's candle

These candles have light and life of their own.
They do not take light from each other, nor from *(Name).*
They simply create between them more light and warmth for
    living.

Parents:
We commit ourselves
to keeping the light of our loving care
burning close to the life of *(Name)*,
and to give to *her/him* and receive from *her/him* as *she/he* journeys
    on *her/his* way.

A bowl of earth is placed near the candles

Leader:
This child does not live alone with us,
but is already a citizen of this earth, among its peoples.

**We commit ourselves to try to create here
a safe and just place for *her/him* and for all children.**

BLESSING
Around this child are gathered many hopes for *her/his* well-being.
Let us each say words
which express the gift for *her/his* future
which we would like to bring to *(Name)*.

The people offer their words or prayers for the child

Now let us place in this 'time capsule'
a message or a symbol or a gift
which we would like *her/him* to have when *she/he* is 14 years old.

The people bring their gifts

Let us gather around this loved child.

The people do so

Parents or person presiding (placing their hands on child's head):
(Name),we will always love you.
With all our hearts and minds and strength,
we bless you on this day and all the days ahead.
May all that is loving in the universe surround you,
all that is strong and true and free walk with you
and your life be filled with joy.

Or:

(Name), we will always love you.
With all our hearts and minds and strength,
we bless you on this day and all the days ahead.
May God, the greater Parent, surround you with love,
Christ Jesus walk beside you all the way
and the Spirit dance in life ahead of you.
Amen.

Toast to the child

JOIN THE DANCE
In a new century

For this service you will need

- *A swirl of different coloured cloths arranged on the table or altar with a cross at its centre*

CALL TO WORSHIP

The years, the centuries, the millennia,
are but your small moments, O God:
moments in which your life always lives and dances on.

This life is passed from heart to heart, soul to soul, life to life:
affirming its presence in each recreation.

You, O God, will never leave us, nor forsake us.
**The music of your truth
will echo among us forever.
We will join the dance of life!**

PRAYER OF INVOCATION

Come, eternal God, come, Jesus Christ, born of us.
Come, Holy Spirit, light and joy, healing and hope.
We wait in faith to be sustained
in the great hope to which we are called as the people of God.
Be with us in this time and place and lift our hearts to you.
Amen.

PRAYER OF CONFESSION

Dear God, if people tell us that the final judgement is upon us,
we are tempted to believe them.
So great is the groaning of the whole creation
and so wide the signs of the triumph of sinfulness,
so powerful the deathliness around us in this day.

Voices name some of the current events and situations

If our capacity for faith is running low,
please understand why that might be so, O God.
If we are tempted to give power to those who confuse us
with their commitments to one act of honesty
while they destroy and betray the greater good,
renew us with your grace, O God.
When we lose sight of the dancing which lies below the grieving
and give strength to forces which tell us that you are no longer
  God,
forgive us and open our eyes to the beauty of your faithfulness.
For we ask this in the name of Christ,
Amen.

WORDS OF ASSURANCE

Our God looks on the heart with compassion and truth.
This is to be trusted. So is the witness of the faithful down the
  ages.
Do not be afraid! We are forgiven!
Thanks be to God.
Amen.

READINGS

2 Samuel 6.1–5, 12b–19
Psalm 24
Ephesians 1.3–14
Mark 6.14–29

SERMON

AFFIRMATION OF FAITH

In response to the word, let us affirm our faith:

We will affirm the voices of justice
for they are the soundings of God.
We will raise the announcements of hope
for they are the songs of the Creator.
We will celebrate the actions of grace
for they are the footprints of the Spirit.

We will watch for the winds of love,
moving gently among the grieving.
We will listen for the stories of wonder,
speaking softly from the hearts of the humble.
We will breathe in the dreams for a new day
for they rise like everlasting incense
from deep in the soul of God.

In our present, our past and our future,
God is the God of all that is.
This we believe.
From this will we live.

PRAYER OF INTERCESSION

Living God, we believe that our prayers are heard,
rising like small puffs of hope
towards the mystery of your divine life –
where you will touch the centre of our deepest longings.

Give us new faith in the face of the realities which we see around
    us,
give us courage to go on when good seems to be defeated
and ways of knowing where your life still goes on.

In childlike trust we share these longings with you now.

The people, or some previously approached people, share their deepest
longings for the church and the world

Hold us in the hollow of your hand, O God.
We know there is nothing beyond your concern

and nothing too human to be beneath your attention.
Your love is never less than our love.
Our grieving is never more than your grieving.

Like the rays of the rising sun,
reach out towards us and warm our life.
Like the tenderness of a grandparent, wise with experience
and gentle with our vulnerable smallness:
Hold us in this time, O God,
and bring us to a different day.
Amen.

COMMISSIONING

Go as those who see beyond death into risen life
and point to this life in the world
that all may move from cynicism and despair
to take hold of the great hope.
Go as the dancing life of God in the world!

The cloths are taken from the table and children or young people run
with them above their heads down the aisle

BENEDICTION

Go in peace to live among the signs of God.
And may Christ Jesus break bread at your table,
the Creator spread a cloth for the feast
and the Spirit dance in the centre of your gathering.
Amen.

↜

LET US SING!

This is a liturgy which has as its focus the call to sing in Ephesians 5.19.
In the Revised Common Lectionary this passage stands alongside the
John 6 passage about eating the flesh and drinking the blood of Jesus,
which many of us find difficult to hear. To connect singing with those
who have taken into themselves the very life of Jesus Christ can be
helpful. The prayers for the service are here, but obviously they will be
made significant by the introduction of singing and music, as
appropriate for your context.

CALL TO WORSHIP

This is the moment of singing, singing in joy.
Let us sing to our God!

This is the time to add to the melodies resounding in creation.
Let us sing to our God!

This is the hour of celebration for life in all its fullness.
Let us make music as an echo of Miriam and David
and of all the voices and notes of joy down the years!
Let us sing to our God, for this is the God of our salvation.

INVOCATION

Be found within us, loving Jesus,
flesh of our flesh, bone of our bone,
the one who did not fear to enter our every human reality.
Be found in the common bread we break and the cup we share
as we take within us the life which you offer, the saving life of
  God.
Amen.

CONFESSION

God of joy, even though we sing hymns in worship to you
sometimes our lives do not reflect
the life of passion and abundance that you lived.
We may even stand out in the community
as those who are eminently serious,
who don't often lead the songs of celebration among the people.

Silent reflection

If our songs have become a ritual
rather than overflowing from the heart:
Forgive us, O God.
or sung **Kyrie**

If we have lost the lightness of soul,
the attractiveness of people within whom you live:
Forgive us, O God.
or sung **Kyrie**

If songs are things we argue about
rather than an echo of your joyful soul:
Forgive us, O God, and break forth into our life.
Amen.
or sung **Kyrie**

WORDS OF ASSURANCE

The song in creation goes ringing around the world in every time.
It is always there for us to receive.
We are always invited to join in its refrains of praise.
Come, lift your hearts in hope and faith!

Sung: **Gloria** *or* **Hallelujah!**

READINGS

1 Kings 2.10–12, 3.3–14
Psalm 111
Ephesians 5.15–20
John 6.51–58

SERMON

Maybe in music and song, or stories of how the hymns came to be as they flowed from the hearts of those who experienced the Christ enfleshed among them and within them

AFFIRMATION

Let us affirm our faith by singing, as have people down the ages.

DOXOLOGY

(Sung)

PRAYER OF INTERCESSION

Even as we sing our songs of hope and joy, O God,
we know they will be an offence
to those in whose life there is little justice:
those who are wounded by life,
the lonely, the people devastated in wars,
the hungry, exploited and homeless.
May our songs energize
your costly life within us, Jesus Christ.

Your life was never a lifting of the hands and heart
in false happiness,
a pumping up of the soul in cheap notes of cheerfulness.
**May our songs energize
your costly life within us, Jesus Christ.**

Sung response

Sometimes when we try to live with your life
the task seems endless and relentless, O God.
When we sing into the wildernesses and deserts
of the tough journey:
**May our songs energize
your costly life within us, Jesus Christ.**

Sung response

For you are the song and the singer,
you are the melody of truth and compassion,
you are the harmony of unity and reconciliation.
**Sing in us as we go, Jesus Christ, who is all in all.
Amen.**

Sung response

COMMISSIONING

Go as those whose voice sounds among the people in kindness
  and delight.
Carry the music of God to those whose life is without a song.
Go in confidence and faith.

BLESSING

And may God lighten the skies around you,
Christ Jesus feed your life in every meal
and the Spirit be at prayer in your beginnings and endings.
Amen.

ALL CREATURES, GREAT AND SMALL

This is not intended to be a re-run of a Vicar of Dibley episode with animals leaping all over the church – unless that appeals to you, of course! It is, nevertheless, an attempt to express the joy we have in creatures, great and small. Which pet-lover hasn't a story to tell?

We once had a strong and well-organized tomcat called Sausage who ate tinned cat food at our house, lightly poached whiting and eggflips with the old woman next door and slept in the lounge of the next house down by going through their cat door. Sausage was very territorial and usually no cat dared to put a whisker on his large territory. One day, I looked out of the window and there was Sausage eating his food with eight other cats sitting around him in a respectful circle. He ate his food calmly, then the other cats dispersed. That was the very last time we saw Sausage. Who knows what that was about?

Preparation

Ask each person in the congregation to bring a photo of their favourite creature – pet or wild, animal, bird, reptile or fish. If you wish, ask some people, possibly children or old people, to tell some short stories about a pet or special animal.

For this service you will need

- *Something like a large paper or cloth on which to mount the photos*
- *Blu-tack or circles of sticky tape to mount them*

CALL TO WORSHIP

God is the Creator,
with an imagination gathered into a universe of wonder.
In every living thing is a glimpse of God,
in every sound and song is a note of God,
in every touching warmth between us
is a mystery of the love of God.
Let us worship God!

CONFESSION

Sadly, we do not always love and respect your creatures, O God.

Silent reflection

When we take more resources than we need for our survival,
in excessive consuming of other living creatures
and the things which they need for their lives,
and lightly using them for our own purposes
then just as easily disposing of them:
Forgive us, Creator God.

If we have degraded
the environment which they need for their survival,
consuming it and destroying it for our own plans,
so that life for the more fragile creatures is ended
or threatened:
Forgive us, Creator God.

If we have not loved as we should
those creatures which are dependent on us,
seeing ourselves as having dominion over them,
rather than responsibility for them,
making of ourselves lesser creatures
because we have failed to live in true community with them:
Forgive us, Creator God,
and show us your vision for the harmony of all that you have
    made.
Amen.

WORDS OF ASSURANCE
Behold, God is making all things new!
Before they break from the bud, they are announced to us.
We may be part of God's new creation in Jesus Christ.
We are forgiven.
Thanks be to God!

READINGS

SERMON

This can include stories from people about their experiences with creatures

THANKSGIVING

Praise be to God for all the wonder of the creation!
Praise be to God for all creatures, great and small!
For which special creature will we give our thanks to God?
Let us bring our photos and place them in the centre as a
   celebration
of all the different gifts of God to us in the creatures that we love.

The people bring their photos and attach them to the cloth or paper

Thanks be to God for all the love given to us by creatures,
for their fun and playing with us, their touching life with us.
Thanks be to God for all this love and beauty
and these marvellous additions to our life!

Let us sing:
A hymn like 'All things bright and beautiful'

PRAYER OF INTERCESSION

Children could be asked to bring their special prayers for creatures, or:

Dear God, guard all that you have made.
Inspire us to understand better the life of the whole creation
so that we can cherish it as you do.
We believe that you are a God who notices the falling of a
   sparrow.
Give us hearts which notice all life that is around us
as though we have a sacred task to keep it because it has been
   made by you
and for the joy of future generations.
At this time, we especially think of these parts of your creation
   which are at risk.

The people bring their prayers

Keep safe all that you have made, O God,
and help us to care for it as you would have us do.
Amen.

BLESSING

Go into the world and see it with fresh eyes
as God's good and great creation.
And may we find new companions on the way,
more love in small things than we had felt before
and the joy of the life of the universe in all its Godly
    harmonies.
Amen.

‿

WE CELEBRATE LEADERSHIP
For those ending training for leadership in some task
or organization

For this service you will need

- *A large candle and a basket of flowers, placed on a long coloured cloth
  which is draped from a table and down on to the floor like a pathway
  towards the group*
- *A bowl of salt water ('tears')*
- *Small candles and tapers*
- *Glasses of wine or other drink for everyone*

ENDING AND BEGINNING

This is a moment of closure
as we end this particular way of journeying with each other.
It is also a time when we celebrate
the new ways of being together
in friendship and networking into the future.

THE GIFTS

It is a moment of naming as significant
the gifts we have received here
and the gifts we have given to each other
over this time of our meeting.

The gifts we have received
are like flowers on the way, signs of the blossoming of life.

Let us place flowers on this cloth as we remember those gifts
in our walking together on this brief pathway.

The people do so

A GRIEVING

The leadership journey is always the entry into the openness
of new possibilities for ourselves and for others,
but sometimes there are steps we cannot take.
There are fears within us,
prices we feel we cannot pay,
forces against us which are too powerful
and timings which seem not right for us.
There is a grieving in this moment.
We will place this bowl of 'tears' in the centre
and acknowledge our grieving.

*The bowl is placed and the people reflect in silence or share their grieving
with each other*

NEW POSSIBILITIES

For those who lead, there are always some new possibilities.
It is like seeing a new light before us, among us or in ourselves.
This light may be fragile or strong,
clear and bright, or just a small spark of insight,
but to be a leader is to expect to see it in each next moment.
If you can see a new possibility before you
for your contribution to the well-being of the world,
I invite you to select a candle, light it, and name that possibility.

The people do so

Leadership is to participate in a dream
for humankind and all that is.
It is to believe that we see a dream
and can give it shape and voice,
that we can give it energy and courage,
that we can give it freedom and vivid colours.

It is a dream for each and all,
for the present and the future.

It expands the horizons of humanity into a new distance
of love and justice, freedom, imagination and peace.
It calls us to live with the gravest responsibility and the deepest
joy.

We are the people of many dreams.
Let us look on each other's faces,
celebrate the things of hope which we have discovered,
and lift our glasses.

The people are given glasses of wine

To a new dream, for us and for the world!

In This Hour, Let us Grieve

The hidden side of our inner life,
with its unseen tears running along like an underground stream,
is beautiful,
but its waters are sometimes scalding hot,
or stingingly salty,
or running as though they will never stop and will get deep and
   drowning,
or almost dry because no one is crying for us,
or because we can't cry for ourselves.

THE HOUR OF LOSS

This is a liturgy to gather up and acknowledge many different forms of loss – death, health, fitness, youth, career, home, country of origin, child, status, hope, confidence, relationship – anything which is now a blank space within us.

For this service you will need

- *A long purple cloth*
- *A large white candle*
- *A number of small candles and tapers*
- *A basket containing some cut flowers*

OPENING

Within most of us there is a mourning,
an empty space which was once filled
or which we expected to fill,
a sense of ourselves which is no longer there,
a way of being and living which has gone.
Within us there is a loss,
a grieving for something held precious.

In this moment we claim the dignity of our human journey,
our travelling with a grief.
In self-respect we claim it for ourselves
and in compassion, we honour it in others.
In faith, we lay it before a loving God.
It is like a white light which burns within us
in the dignity of our living.

A purple cloth is spread and a large candle lit

RESPECTING THE LOSS

Sometimes loss is white with sharp pain,
sometimes it is white with emptiness

and sometimes it is a white and gentle warm light
which starts to fill the space left by the loss.

Silent reflection

What are the losses which we want to honour before each other
and before our God today?
What do we want to bring for naming as significant,
worthy of our awareness, and worthy of our care?
As we sing quietly *(or listen to this music)*
anyone who wishes to bring forward a loss in their lives
is invited to light a small candle and place it on the cloth.
If you wish to name the loss out loud, feel free to do so,
or you may wish to simply name it in your heart.

*The people quietly sing something like a Taizé chant, e.g. 'By night we
travel in darkness' or 'Bless the Lord, my soul', or a quiet Kyrie as people
come forward to light the candles*

READING AND/OR REFLECTION

THE COMFORTING

Let us place these, our losses, in the hands of God.
Dear God, you who cried when you lost a friend,
who wept over Jerusalem,
who asked friends to stay with you
while you struggled with your life,
please stay with us now, holding us in your love.
Cover our lives with the fragrant oil of your healing,
send your Spirit to comfort us in our grief,
and fill our emptiness with new things.
Gather our scattered lives into a community of love,
where loss can be shared and gifts can be given
for the easing of mourning.
We pray these prayers in confidence,
for you are our restoration and the renewal of our hope.
Amen.

BLESSING

Let us bless all these things we have lost,
covering them round with flowers,

so that they know they are cherished
and we know that we are cherished,
never left alone to grieve.

The people put flowers around the candles and give flowers to each other

Go in peace,
And may the loving Parent God surround you with love,
Christ Jesus hold out arms of healing towards you,
and the Spirit gather you into a new day.
Amen.

~

CLOSING THE SPACE
Between us and God

This is a ritual to help people reflect on the things which stand between them and connecting with their God. These things are usually paralysing our life to some extent, even though we try to push them away. It assumes that, when we experience a sense of wilderness, desert, emptiness, chaos, or dark night of the soul, there is really something in that space, however we name the space. It is likely to be something related to anger, pain or guilt, or a combination of these. The invitation is to 'respect' whatever it is that is there, and to honour its presence in our authentic life with a grieving. Grieving makes no judgement.

For this ritual you will need

- *A long blue cloth – if is streaked with different shades of blue, like water, all the better*
- *Enough pieces of blue ribbon for everyone – different shades of blue – to be placed by people's chairs.*
- *A bowl or basket of smooth coloured stones, cut flowers, small branches of leaves, pieces of brightly coloured paper or ribbon, and other small brightly coloured things, like glass fish, frogs, little paper boats.*

INTRODUCTION

All of us have barriers between ourselves and God.

Sometimes they gather in such power that we experience a terrible space between ourselves and God, a chaos or emptiness within and alienations between ourselves and other people.

This can take many forms, like:
an emptiness like a desert or silence, a hollowness,
a feeling as though we are trapped in a chaotic wilderness,
a dark lowness of spirit,
a paralysis, a going around in endless circles, sometimes in the
    same circle,
a lack of energy, everything is an act of will, an effort,
a lack of hope, a tiredness.

However we name that separation, that space, there is always something in it, something which stays there until it is recognized and owned.

I am not going to suggest today that as soon as we acknowledge something it goes, or it is healed, or that we can immediately forgive and give up our anger and the pain of our wounding. In many cases that would be to be less than respectful of the tough reality of our lives.

THE INVITATION

Today, I invite you to believe that
if we cover what is there with grieving,
it will narrow the space between us and ourselves,
us and each other,
and us and God.

THE NAMING

This blue cloth is the hidden side of our inner life,
with its unseen tears running along like an underground stream.
It is beautiful,
but its waters are sometimes scalding hot,
or stingingly salty,
or running as though they will never stop and will get deep and
    drowning,

or almost dry because no one is crying for us,
or because we can't cry for ourselves.

I invite you stay in the silence and to write on the blue ribbons by
your chair what lies within that unseen, unrespected, unhealed
life for you.

You may want to write a word like 'anger', or 'wounding', or you
may want to be more specific, or you may simply want to place
your ribbon with no words.

Or this symbolic action may have no meaning for you and you
would rather share in the grieving of others.

A silence is kept

If you wish and when you are ready,
you are invited to place your ribbon on the cloth
as part of the many streams of grieving in humankind.

The people do so

THE GRIEVING

Let us view this cloth and especially our own ribbon of tears
with deep concern,
with genuine respect,
with recognition for its authentic truth about ourselves,
its courage in lying there for us to see.

A space for respectful reflection

READINGS, POEMS, STORIES OR MUSIC

THE CHERISHING

The reality of the things which grieve us,
which make spaces of pain in our lives,
cannot be removed in a moment,
but we can put cherishing things around them
so that we travel on in a different way.
We could put smooth and beautiful stones for the tears to pass
    over,
flowers or green beauty alongside,

small streaks of colour in the water, reflections of passing
    kindness,
or little new signs of life which sail along on the water,
even though it goes running on in its grief.

The people cherish the tears of life

MOVING ON

We will not pretend that all this part of our pained life is now at
    ease,
nor that our bound self is set free,
our woundedness forgiven, our fears and chaos ended
and our spirit at peace.
We will simply leave all this truth about ourselves
respectfully where it is for this hour
and move a little further,
coming back to attend to it when we can,
today or another day.

WE MAY MEET OUR GOD

We are not alone.
All of us share in this human reality.
None of us has no hidden tears.
That is our strength as we travel this life together.
That is the beginning of grace.

There is a God who has also travelled this pathway,
who also shed tears
and experienced all that we experience,
was tempted like us, angry like us,
afraid like us and wounded like us, even to the death.
This God waits to meet us in the next moment.

Silent reflection

Go in peace and grace.
Amen.

It is good to have something like supper or a meal after this

HEALING SERVICE
For those grieving the termination of a pregnancy

People decide to terminate a pregnancy for all sorts of reasons. This service is for those who, even though they believe that they made the best choice they could, still grieve the ending of something which had begun.

For this service you will need

- *A table and long red cloth*
- *Flowers placed on the table ready for placing on the cloth*
- *A bowl of fragrant oil*

OPENING SENTENCES

Turn your face towards us, O God,
even though we sometimes hide our faces from you.
Hold out your healing robe towards our hands,
for we stand hidden in the crowd of life
and dare not ask for healing.
Hold us in the hollow of your hand, O God,
that we may believe we are loved.
Amen.

CONFESSION

We are here before you, O God of grace,
you who are the source of life,
all life, and our life.
We are here to grieve that we could not sustain
a life begun in us,
that we could not bring it to birth.
O God, the bleeding of our bodies and souls,
as we think of that
life goes on as it did in the woman who was haemorrhaging
all those years ago,
the one who believed she was unclean.
It is like a stream of pain which will not stop, O God.

A long red cloth is placed from the table towards the people and a silence is kept

God, who sees into the depths of our hearts,
believe us when we say that we did our best
at the time of our decision to end this fragile life.
Help us to believe that you know us
and walked within our life at that time,
travelling that hard journey with us,
understanding our human weakness.

A silence is kept, or people speak of the story of their lives around the decision

Come to us, God of forgiveness and love,
heal us and give us peace.
Amen.

READING

LAYING TO REST
Let us remember this brief life begun in us,
remember it with love and grieving for its ending.
Let us place flowers on the cloth of our bleeding
in memory of that life.

The people place flowers

Let us remember our own brokenness
and grieve for the things which felt as though they died in us
as that small life ended.

If appropriate the people may say words which express this

The small life which was begun in us
is now gathered into the larger life of God.
Here this life will be kept safe forever
and be renewed by its Creator.
It will be gathered under the warm wings of the Spirit
and will never be left or forsaken
because the little and the least are loved of God.

The grieving people are asked to kneel and those supporting gather around

Let us lay down the carrying of this life
which has been for us a burden of sadness and guilt.
Leave that life in the hands of God.
Trust that God loves you and forgives you
and receive in faith the oil of joy for your mourning,
the oil of anointing for your healing.

The people are anointed and then invited to join the circle with their friends

PRAYER

Either prayers from the friends, or:

O God, travel with us all into a new day.
We are all your human people,
all have fallen short of your hope for us
and our hope for ourselves.
Lift up our hearts in hope and praise!
Lift up our souls in newness,
like buds breaking into a new blossoming.
**We will go forth
as those who have received much
and will now give much
in love and forgiveness to others.
Thanks be to God,
who is our salvation from day to day,
our hope and our grace.
Amen.**

BLESSING

Go in peace,
to bear witness to the love of God.
And may God the Creator go on creating in us,
Jesus our Saviour walk before us in each new day
and the Spirit dance with life within us.
Amen.

MUTUAL CONFESSION AT THE CLOSURE OF A MINISTRY
Between the departing minister and the people

These prayers of mutual confession may be added to a service of farewell, which is customarily presided over by a regional leader (e.g. Chairperson of Presbytery or Synod) or sometimes a congregational leader.

MUTUAL CONFESSION

Minister:
God of grace,
if I have ever betrayed my calling
and left the people without the word,
forgive me.
If I have failed to offer in faith the gifts of ministry
which you have given me to share with others,
forgive me.
If I have not recognized and affirmed
the gifts of ministry in others,
forgive me.
If there are other things
which stand between me and this congregation
which would prevent us
from truly offering to each other your peace,
forgive me and reconcile me to yourself
and to the people of God in this place,
in the power of the Holy Spirit.
Amen.

The members of the congregation:
Gracious God,
if we have refused to receive the word
and the gifts of ministry
which you have offered to us in *(Name),*
forgive us.
If we have asked of our minister
more than our due
and have failed to take our place alongside this ministry
as the Body of Christ in all its fullness,

forgive us.
If there are things which still stand between us and *(Name)*
which prevent us passing the peace in spirit and in truth,
forgive us and reconcile us in the power of the Holy Spirit.
Amen.

ASSURANCE OF PARDON

Presiding minister or leader:
All that is past is now gathered into the grace of God.
We are never other than frail human beings.
We all fall short of the glory of God.
The miracle is that we are forgiven
and that in some special moments, God is indeed seen in us.
Thanks be to God!

FOR A BATTERED WOMAN
A service of healing for a woman wounded by domestic violence

For this service you will need

- *A long red cloth*
- *Three small crosses and one larger cross*
- *A large candle*
- *A garland of flowers*
- *Fragrant oil for anointing*
- *A purple or brightly coloured scarf*

OPENING

We gather here
as those who surround this woman
with our love,
as those who are part of a society
in which violence still lives
and as those who announce that this need not be,
it must not be

and that we will add the name of God
to our efforts to see that it will one day end.

WE HAVE SEEN
We have seen the bleeding, the bruising in this woman's life,
the bleeding and bruising of her body, mind, heart and soul.

A long red cloth is spread from the woman towards the people

We have seen her trust betrayed
in her relationships,
(a small cross is placed on the cloth)
in her perceptions of herself,
(a small cross is placed on the cloth)
in the way things should be in this world,
(a small cross is placed on the cloth)
and her faith in a loving God shaken and trembling,
sometimes destroyed.

A larger cross is placed at the head of the cloth

GRIEVING
O God of Calvary,
the One whose friends called out 'Crucify',
and kissed the dangerous enemies
or ran away and left you alone,
the One who felt the nails go into hands
and sword into side,
we pray to you in grief for this our friend.
O God, we are so stricken as we face
what has happened to her as she tried to live her life
in faithfulness to normal expectations
that her home would be her sanctuary.

We grieve that, even to this day,
parts of our society still give subtle permission
for violence against women
within relationships,
as though there could be good reasons
for brutality and the exercise of violent power.

We grieve that so many women are still trapped in this,
staying in terror in situations which invite them
to assume responsibility for their own victimization,
or because they cannot find a way
to protect both themselves and their children
or to see another way forward for themselves.
In silence, we contemplate this tragedy.

A silence is kept

We know we are not alone, O God.
We know that you grieve with us,
you are angry alongside our anger
and you long with us for violence to stop.
Come to us with your power for love
and recreate the world with us.
Amen.

READINGS OF HOPE

Suggested:
Isaiah 42.4–10
Isaiah 61.1–4
Revelation 21.1–6

GIFTS FOR HEALING

The woman is invited to stand at the end of the red cloth and the people gather around her

Voice 1:
We will give you a garland instead of ashes:
This is our gift to you for your new future.

A garland of flowers is placed around her

Voice 2:
We will give you the oil of gladness instead of mourning:
This is our gift to you for your new future.

The woman is anointed with fragrant oil

Voice 3:
We will give you a mantle of praise instead of a faint spirit:
This is our gift to you for your new future.

A purple or brightly coloured scarf is placed on her shoulders

These are the signs of the love of God for you,
the company of the presence of God as you walk forward.
These are the signs of our love for you
and our company as you walk forward
and move towards healing and strength.

We surround you with warmth.
The signs of your wounding and betrayal
will be transformed into the power of God for a new day,
and the bright strength of never being alone again.

The small crosses are gathered around the large cross and placed on the table with a candle and the red cloth is made into a circle around the woman

BLESSING
Go in hope and faith into the next days,
and may God recreate our future,
Christ Jesus leap free in risen life among us
and the Spirit heal and comfort us all
in body, mind, heart and soul.
Amen.

Music, as people move away or take the woman for a meal

In This Hour, Let us Pause

Today we pause to honour ourselves
as people who are precious in the eyes of God,
in the eyes of each other
and respected by ourselves.

Today we give space
in the rush of human existence
to feel what we feel,
find the hope within us
and be open to the receiving of love.

WHO ARE WE?

This is a ritual intended to model for people a process for getting in touch with themselves. Oddly enough, especially when we are under pressure, we often lose a sense of who we are and how we are feeling about things. The imaging of God also usually tells us something about ourselves. If this is part of a day of retreat, it comes well after the ritual 'Closing the Space' (see page 29). If it is for a multifaith or secular group of people, the references to God can be changed to things like 'higher power' or 'centre of the universe' or 'the forces for love and good beyond ourselves', or in some cases removed altogether.

Preparation

If this ritual is part of some hours together and is to be held in a suitable environment, the finding of the images for oneself and for God can be part of the day. If it is a briefer event and in a more limited environment, people can be asked to bring something which images themselves and their current image for God: an object, prepared words, or music.

For this ritual you will need

- *A focus area in the centre or at the front, with a table and cloth for the placing of the images*
- *Wine or fruit juice and small cups for the toast, either on a tray to be passed around or in a jug for pouring*

INTRODUCTION

If this is part of a period together in a place where people can find images to bring to the ritual:

This is a day when we pause to reconnect with ourselves, when we respect that who we are is important.

I invite you to spend a time alone *(specify)*, to move around this place and see if you can find an object or something you can describe which reminds you of yourself at this moment.

After you have done that, see if you can find some image which reminds you of who God is for you at this time or who you would like God to be for you. This is not your total picture of God, just one face of God.

If you are not the sort of person who images things, think of another way of telling yourself who you are and who your God is at this time, like writing some words or thinking what music you would hear.

Bring both these images back with you.

When the people return:

I now invite you to cluster in groups of four *(or appropriate number)*, hold what you have brought and share as much or as little about the images you have chosen as you feel comfortable doing.

After *(time)* we will regather as a group and bring ourselves and our images for God together.

OPENING

Today we pause to honour ourselves
as people who are precious in the eyes of God,
in the eyes of each other
and respected by ourselves.

Who we are at this moment is significant.
Our human being is valuable,
whether it is fragile or strong,
fearful or brave,
clear or confused,
wise or foolish,
growing and moving
or resting and staying.
We all deserve to be seen and known,
especially by ourselves.

NAMING WHO WE ARE

I invite you now to bring forward your imaging of yourself
and to place it on the cloth.

The people do so

Each one is valuable in its authentic life
and together we form a whole at this moment
as a gathering of graceful, warmly human strength and
    giftedness.

Let us look at who we are:

Silence or quiet music for reflection

Let us lift a glass to the beauty of humankind in ourselves!

*Wine or fruit juice or something else which is good to drink is passed
around in small cups*

Just because we exist,
just because we try our best to live,
just because together we could do and be anything we choose,
let us drink to each and to all:
To each and to all!

THE NAMING OF GOD

Our naming for God at this time
is a revealing to ourselves of longings and hopes
about the power for good beyond ourselves,
and the resource for life
which we need and claim as possible.
This imaging may change for us tomorrow,
but today, this is the face of God turned towards us.

Let us bring forward our symbols.
If you wish, say aloud the word which describes your symbol.
Place them around the symbols for ourselves
like a surrounding of support and love,
a cherishing of us.

The people do so

I invite you to move into a circle around this table.

The people do so

Let us look in awe at the possibilities
which have now gathered around our life.

A silence is kept

In the good power in each other
and with this God, brought together in all these namings,
we could survive well.
Maybe we could transform the world!

BLESSING
Go in courage and celebration!
And may all the faces of the Holy God
be turned towards you in love,
the earth itself speak to you of its creativity
and who we are, each and all,
be honoured in our authentic journeys.
Amen.

↜

DECEMBER DIARY
For Advent

These four hours for pausing were prepared with a group of people from the Knox Presbyterian Church of Aotearoa New Zealand.

The goal was to invite the people who lived, worked or stayed in the area around the church to join with some members of the church in a time of pausing and reflection: a meditative time together over four lunchtime periods in the two weeks prior to Christmas. The church members saw this as both a time for themselves and as a way of connecting with the wider community in a sensitive way.

During the carefully prepared and focused time, they hoped that in the busy life before Christmas people would be given space to come into a self-awareness which is caring, sometimes healing, restful and hopeful.

People were encouraged to bring their lunches with them and were offered hospitality with tea and coffee.

A large 'Diary page' was placed on a stand in the foyer of the church with a handwritten entry indicating the theme for the week on the date of the meditation.

There were 'focus chapels' in different parts of the church which imaged the themes of the four meditations which were suitable for ongoing private reflection outside the actual events. The Sunday Advent services also took account of the themes.

People from the community did come to the meditations, a few even joined the church. The 'chapel' area which kept drawing most of the people for meditation was undoubtedly the space for memories and grieving.

◡

A SPACE FOR PEACE
Meditation 1

For this service you will need

- *A 'focus chapel' for peace:*
  A simple peace banner hung as backdrop
  Candles in holders on a stand, with a cloth draped underneath
  A sign placed in a prominent position which reads: 'A Space for Peace: Here you are invited to meditate or pray for peace, peace for yourself, peace for the world'
  Chairs placed in a half-circle
- *Quiet music*
- *A main candle lit on a stand in the centre aisle of the church, with the peace candle unlit beside it*

INTRODUCTION

In the approach to Christmas, the people of this church are offering, for any people who wish to come, a quiet space and a simple way of becoming more aware of their journey in December.

Today, the focus is on pausing for peace in the rush and bustle of life.

We will be listening to music, creating times of silence and focusing on symbols like a candle to help us enter this time of quiet reflection.

You are welcome to come or go as you need, participate as much or as little as you like and to share in tea or coffee afterwards.

Let us keep silent as an entry into this time.

A brief silence is kept

IN THESE DAYS
We are often overwhelmed and distracted by our attempts to prepare for Christmas and all that is involved in this season.

We are pressured by all that needs to be done,
caught in the tide of gift searches and decisions,
sometimes anxious about the cost of it all.
We are often flurried in trying to think what we have missed
and who is needing our attention and care.

ON THIS DAY
Let us commit ourselves to pause, to rest for a time,
to be aware of what we are doing to ourselves
and to enter a time of peaceful reflection.

Let us allow this space, this place, to offer its care to us,
restful in its quiet,
away from the hustle and bustle of our everyday life.

As we hear this quiet music,
let us lay down our lists of things to do,
our concerns and matters for decision,
believing that to do this
is to invite greater clarity and new energy later.

Music

WE ARE NOT ALONE
The lighting of this candle joins us with people around the world who long for peace, all sorts of peace, for all the people.

A brief story of people from another part of the world who long for peace

Christmas is a time when we hope for gifts of peace.
We will light this candle as a sign that we long for peace.
We pray for peace in these days, personal peace, and peace for the
world.

The peace candle is lit

Let us stay in silence and reflect on ways in which we long for
    peace.
Let us be open to insights about the creation of peace
around us and within us at this time.

A silence is kept

Let us carry these candles into a space for people to sit in quiet
and meditate or pray so that more peace may be gathered here
in this busy time.

The candles are carried to the focus chapel for peace

BLESSING

Go in peace,
the peace which passes understanding.
And may the gift of quiet be still within you,
the gift of calm surround your soul
and God walk with you in wisdom and grace.
Amen.

Music

A SPACE FOR MEMORIES AND GRIEVING
Meditation 2

For this service you will need

- A 'focus chapel' for memories and grieving:
  A circle of chairs
  On the floor in the centre a small stand (only a few inches high –
  maybe a couple of books covered with a cloth) for the candle and the
  bowl of 'tears'. Swathed around the candle and bowl some purple and
  blue material – in a circle maybe 2–3 feet wide
  A basket of pieces of mauve paper and a few pens close by
  A sign which reads: 'A Space for Memories and Grieving: Here you
  are invited to stay and remember griefs, losses, loneliness or betrayals
  which make it hard for you, or those you love, to experience the joy of
  Christmas'
  Focus on the bowl of tears and, if you wish, write on the pieces of paper
  provided anything you wish to remember, or any request for prayers,
  and place them in the folds of the cloth
- Quiet music
- A candle on a stand/table in the centre aisle of the church with a bowl
  of 'tears' (salt water) alongside

INTRODUCTION

In the approach to Christmas, the people of this church are
offering, for any people who wish to come, a quiet space and a
simple way of becoming more aware of their journey in
December.

Today, the focus is on pausing to remember in ourselves, or in
others, the life experiences which may bring a sense of loss, grief
or pain into Christmas.

We will be listening to music, creating times of silence and
focusing on symbols to help us enter this time of quiet reflection.

You are welcome to come or go as you need, participate as much
or as little as you like and to share in tea or coffee afterwards.

Let us keep silent as an entry into this time.

A brief silence is kept

IN THESE DAYS

When the focus of the community is on the coming of love into the
    world,
on the expression of that love in families,
on having many friends and people who love us
for the giving and receiving of gifts:

Some of us are not surrounded by love,
some of us have no families, or we are part of families
which are less than expressions of loving relationship.

Some of us are carried into painful awareness of loss,
of the absence of people we have loved,
of loneliness, of betrayals of love,
of cynicism as we survey the activities around us.

Sometimes we would rather that Christmas was past,
but even if we try to pretend that we can avoid its claims upon us,
we dread the day, we look with relief to its ending.

Some of us remember others
for whom Christmas is an ordeal rather than a joy.

ON THIS DAY

We will dare to stay, with our real feelings about the journey
    towards Christmas.
On this day we will grieve for ourselves
or for others
who do not look towards Christmas with hopeful anticipation.

A silence is kept

WE ARE NOT ALONE

This is a bowl of salt water.
It symbolizes the tears of the world and our tears as we approach
Christmas.

The bowl is lifted up

As the music is played, let us enter this honest place of grieving in
    our hearts.
Let us think of ourselves and others.

Music

We will carry this bowl of tears into a space in the church
where people can sit and place around it messages of grieving,
as an invitation for others
to recognize the significance of the pain in some lives at this time
and to invite loving thoughts and prayers for their surrounding.

The candle and bowl are carried into the place of grieving

BLESSING
Go in peace.
And may you be held in the hollow of God's hand
for healing and comfort,
surrounded each day by the presence of love
and covered by the warm bright wings of the Spirit.
Amen.

Music

◡

A SPACE FOR HOPE
Meditation 3

For this service you will need

- *A 'focus chapel' for hope:*
  A Christmas tree
  A stand for the main Christ candle with tapers alongside
  A green cloth spread from the tree
  At intervals on the cloth, flat terracotta bowls of sand with unlit tea
  candles placed in the sand
  A sign nearby which reads: 'A Space for Hope: You are invited to sit
  in quiet, to reflect on the small signs of hope which you see around
  you, and light a small candle to honour that hope'
- *Quiet music*
- *A lit candle on a stand in the centre aisle of the church with a small tea*
  candle alongside

INTRODUCTION

In the approach to Christmas, the people of this church are offering, for any people who wish to come, a quiet space and a simple way of becoming more aware of their journey in December.

Today, the focus is on recognizing the small signs of hope which are present among us.

We will be listening to music, creating times of silence and focusing on symbols like small candles to help us enter this time of quiet reflection.

You are welcome to come or go as you need, participate as much or as little as you like and to share in tea or coffee afterwards.

Let us keep silent as an entry into this time.

A brief silence is kept

IN THESE DAYS

We sometimes find it hard to see the signs of hope around us.
There are so many overwhelming signs of struggle, tragedy and
    suffering,
so many people worried about their futures.

If we look at what lies before us for ourselves and the world,
it sometimes seems that death is more powerful than life,
greed is more common than generosity and kindness
and the idea of hope something that is hard to sustain.

ON THIS DAY

We will pause and discover the fragile signs of hope which we see
    around us.
We will believe that they are there and will survive,
and that we are part of that hope.

The small candle is lit

We will assume that love is stronger than hate,
that life-giving things are more powerful than the things which
    are deathly
and that there are more signs of this than we have paused to
    notice.

WE ARE NOT ALONE

All around the world there are people like us,
sometimes living in much harder places in their lives,
who also long for hope and look with the eyes of faith
to find the signs around them.
We will join our longings with theirs in this moment of pausing
  and reflection.

Music

We will carry this candle as an imaging of the light for the
  discovering of hope
and place it near the Christmas tree,
which is often an image of joy and hope for people.

You are invited to light the very small candles beside it
as signs of delicate hopes you can see around you and, if you
  wish,
to write these signs of hope on the pieces of paper provided
and place them in the sand so that people may read them and be
  encouraged.

The candles are carried to the tree

BLESSING

Go in hope
to discover the fragile and strong hopes which lie around you.
And may the Spirit of God dance in your path,
the Creator rise in life in surprising places
and every turn in the road bring you new possibilities.
Amen.

Music

A SPACE FOR LOVE
Meditation 4

For this service you will need

- *A 'focus chapel' for love:*
  Photos, paintings, symbols of the town and country where the church is displayed on stands or the wall
  Chairs arranged facing the symbols and images
  A stand for the candle with a basket of cut flowers nearby
  Maybe a red cloth swathed around to connect the various images
  A sign which reads: 'A Space for Love: You are invited to pause here and reflect on our town/city and our country as a place where love might come. If you can remember where you have seen love here, please take a flower home with you. While you are here, you may like to pray expectantly for love to be seen here'
- *Quiet music*
- *A lit candle on a stand in the centre aisle of the church with a basket of cut flowers alongside*

INTRODUCTION

In the approach to Christmas, the people of this church are offering, for any people who wish to come, a quiet space and a simple way of becoming more aware of their journey in December.

Today, the focus is on pausing to recognize that love will indeed come to us in this place – our town/city, our country.

We will be listening to music, creating times of silence and focusing on symbols and pictures of our environment to help us enter this time of quiet reflection.

You are welcome to come or go as you need, participate as much or as little as you like and to share in tea or coffee afterwards.

Let us keep silent as an entry into this time.

A brief silence is kept

IN THESE DAYS

We wonder if this is could be the place
where we might see the signs of love and joy and peace
or whether those signs of a loving God among us
are mostly to be found in other places.

Sometimes life here is consumed by a sense of being on our own
    in this place.
Sometimes we are so concentrating on the things which separate
    us
from each other and the rest of the world
that we fail to live with expectation,
to imagine that here, in this place, great love will be offered to us,
in each other and by our God.

A silence is kept

ON THIS DAY

We will look at this space, in the church,
around us in nearby *(name of own country)*
and bring close to ourselves and those we love,
the presence of all that is loving.

Here we will imagine how love could come to us all
and what it would be like to receive that love,
to encourage its blossoming
in our own lives and the life of our community.

Music

WE ARE NOT ALONE

In the creation itself, in this place of *(name)*,
there will be small blossomings of love in the light of Christmas.
We will carry this candle into the corner of the church,
where there are images and flowers from our landscape and our
    town/city.

You are invited to follow and spend some time looking at these
    images
which remind us of the beauty of our country.

Then, if you wish, you may take a flower from the centre or the
    corner of the church
as you remember the signs of love
which you have seen, or the ones for which you long.

*The candle is carried into the corner while some flowers are left in the
centre*

BLESSING

Go safely towards Christmas Day,
trusting that love is moving towards you.
And may the God of love go with you,
the child of Bethlehem touch your life
and gifts of grace lie around you as you journey.
Amen.

Music

↩

In This Hour,
Let us Find our God

In every corner of the world:
the songs of the Creator will break forth in joy!
In the place where we have always been:
the Christ will speak new things before us.
Stay, stay here until it is time to go
as companions on the way.
In heart and mind and soul and strength, let us stay,
for here we may discover the truth in our midst.

WHO DO YOU SAY THAT I AM?

Preparation

A number of people need to be asked to think of their favourite name for God and to bring some symbol which represents that name.

CALL TO WORSHIP

How will we name our God this day?
Wonderful, Counsellor and Prince of peace,
Creator, Redeemer and Sustainer of us all.
How will we name our God this day?
Loving parent who is like a woman in labour who brings us to
    birth
and a man who holds his children in a warm embrace.
How will we name our God this day?
There are no names which give us more than glimpses
of the mystery and the grace of our God.
Let us worship God!

PRAYER OF INVOCATION

We long to find you here with us, O God, who is beyond any
    names.
We dare to hope to discover you in our midst,
for the loving sanctuary of your presence.
Come, make this hour an hour of peace, O God, for we pray in
    faith.
Amen.

CONFESSION

God, who stands before us and asks us to give you a name,
we feel in this moment the awesome demands of that question
    to us.
What if we give you a name of grandeur and holiness
and then go on in our lives as though that makes no difference?

Silent reflection

What if we give you a name which is so small,
so captured by us,
that we delude ourselves into thinking that we know all of you
and can define who you love or do not love,
and when you love or do not love?

Silent reflection

What if we imagine ourselves to be nearly as Godly as you are
because we have dared to say your name
and have stripped you of wonder and mystery?

Silent reflection

Maybe if we remain silent before you,
and take off our shoes in awe,
you will give to us your names
and take away our guilt and fear.

A silence is kept

WORDS OF ASSURANCE

God is the beginning and the end.
God is also known to us in the costly love of Jesus Christ.
Do not be afraid. We may come near to this our God.
Our sin is forgiven.
Thanks be to God!

READINGS
Proverbs 1.20–33
Psalm 19
James 3.1–12
Mark 8.27–38

SERMON

WHO DO YOU SAY THAT I AM?
How will we name our God this day?

*Selected people bring forward images for a name of God of their choosing,
e.g. rock, new birth in a baby, love in a picture, water of life, bread of life*

Have we other names for our God?

The people call them out

We have many names for God.

**This, our God,
comes to us in ways of endless relationship,
in forms and places which are new every day.
God, our God,
is never fully known
but longs to be revealed in us and to us.
Praise be to God!**

DOXOLOGY

(Sung)

PRAYER OF INTERCESSION

God in Jesus Christ, you tried to tell your first disciples
what it would be like to follow you.
You gave to them and to us an image of faithfulness
that always confronts us, even when we pray.
Give to us a larger vision of your hope for the church and the
    world.
Give us hearts full of compassion
and a preparedness to hold high your cross in the bringing in of
    your reign.
We wait on your inspiration in this time and this place.

A silence is kept

We bring our longings to you for the church and the world.

The people bring their longings

O God, if we have the faith to pray
for things we have not seen, for justices which rarely happen,
it is because before us we have the witness of your life and
    death,
the promise lived out as you followed your cross to the end
and leapt free of its power
and will sustain forever the forces of love and grace.

We commit our lives to be your people if you will be our God,
one in three persons, blessed Trinity.
Amen.

COMMISSIONING

Go, carry the name of Jesus into the world.
Go and name God in every place.
Go, and be the witnesses so that all the world will ask
for the name of the God who we serve!

BLESSING

And may Jesus Christ truly be our God,
the One who was in the beginning truly be our Creator
and the Spirit live in vivid life among us all.
Amen.

⌐

THERE WILL BE NO BARRIERS
Between us and God

For this service you will need

- *A large candle to be carried and placed on a stand among the people*
- *A 'veil' to be placed around the candle to dim its light – this could be a plain lampshade or a piece of filmy cloth held around the candle by two people*

CALL TO WORSHIP

Come, come in faith:
For our God is faithful.

Come, come, with hands stretched out:
For there are no barriers between us and the Christ.

Come, come, in love:
**For this is the God who moves towards us,
each of us, all of us.
Let us worship God!**

A candle is carried towards the people

PRAYER OF INVOCATION

Be found here with us, Spirit of God, discovered in our midst
     again,
for we are your disciples of today,
and we invite your knowing of our hopes and fears,
your entering of our longing hearts.
Break down the barriers which we place between us and your
     presence,
for we long to be with you and experience your grace.
Amen.

CONFESSION

Healing God,
sometimes we place a veil of separation between you and
     ourselves.
There are many reasons for this, O God.

Silent reflection as the candle is veiled

It is sometimes hard for us to understand
the pattern of your healing
when you respond to our prayers.
Sometimes it feels as though you don't respond at all
and we worry about our lack of faith and our worthiness.

Silent reflection

If we no longer dare to ask things of you:
Forgive us, O God.

If we fear to be disappointed:
Forgive us, O God.

If we would rather keep you distant
so that you cannot call us away from our illness or our guilt,
because it is easier to be cared for than to take up our beds and
     walk:
Forgive us, O God.

If we are choosing to be victims forever as a way of life,
giving power to those who have wounded us, rather than to you:
Forgive us, O God.

When we turn our faces away from the possibility of your gifts,
or assume that they are ours alone:
**Forgive us and open our lives to your renewal and healing,
O God.
In the name of Jesus Christ,
Amen.**

WORDS OF ASSURANCE

Come to God in faith.
In Jesus Christ, the veil is stripped away from the love of God!

The veil is lowered and placed around the foot of the candle

We will receive the gift of the Holy Spirit, the comforter.
This is the promise in Jesus Christ.
On this day, it is yours, it is ours!
Thanks be to God!

READINGS

2 Samuel 1.1, 17–27
Psalm 130
2 Corinthians 8.7–15
Mark 5.21–43

SERMON

AFFIRMATION OF FAITH

Let us respond to the word and affirm our faith:

**The veil has been torn away from the holy of holies.
God is shown to us in Jesus Christ
and we know this God as grace.**

**The dimness of doubt is over our own lives,
but God has shone a new light over all creation,
the revealing light of Christ,
the healing flame of the Spirit,
the renewing sun of the Creator.**

**In this faith we will live in hope,
believing that we may choose to stand**

within the sanctuary of a place made Godly forever
by the One who walked this life with us.
Christ has died.
Christ is risen.
Christ will come again.
Nothing can separate us from this love.

OFFERING

PRAYER OF INTERCESSION
Let us dream of a world
which is so close to God that transforming healing is possible.
What would it look like?
What would change around us?
What would change in our life as a congregation?

The people describe their hopes

Take these our dreams and make them real, O God,
and create in us visions beyond that which we have yet seen.

Who around us in this day would be reaching with trembling
    hand
to touch the Body of Christ?

The people say the names of people or groups

O loving Jesus, we pray for all these people.
We pray that we will never betray their hopes in the love of your
    church.

We too come with fragile faith,
never enough to encompass your own longings for us.
Bring forth in us dependence on you,
the confidence to pray,
and the commitment to gather all people
nearer to your power for good.

Create in us your body of healing love,
a safe place for all who would come,
a sanctuary of transparent peace

in a groaning and painful world.
For we ask these things in faith,
Amen.

COMMISSIONING

We are the Body of Christ.
It is towards us that the people will come for hope and healing,
believing that the healing Christ is to be found here.
Go and take up the sacred task for this day.

BENEDICTION

Go in peace and walk together with the Christ.
And may our lives be filled with faith,
brave in the hope of the Spirit
and close to the healing hand of God.
Amen.

⌇

BE OPEN

CALL TO WORSHIP

God of the unexpected,
God who crashes through our assumptions:
We worship you.

God, whose friends break through the boundaries,
of preconceived ideas and rules:
We worship you.

God, whose life is written in bold strokes of love
beyond anything which we can predict or dream:
We come to worship you in spirit and in truth!

PRAYER OF INVOCATION

Come to us, O God of surprising grace.
Break into the places in our lives which we think are not worthy of
    your entry,
and show to us the measure of your love for us.

Break through into newness in all our life together, O God,
in the wonder of your transforming presence.
Amen.

CONFESSION

Sometimes, O God, we become people who expect nothing new.
We think we can predict all that we will find in ourselves,
in each other and in people who we decide have nothing to offer.

Silent reflection

When we stereotype groups of people,
prejudging who they might be and what they might do
or shutting them out of your generosity:
Challenge our closed hearts, O God.

If we believe that there is nothing more to be discovered
in this part of your church because we have seen it for a long time:
Challenge our closed minds, O God.

When we think that we know the limits of what you can do,
and tread our life as though there are few new possibilities
    nearby:
**Challenge our closed souls, O God, and forgive our smallness
    of faith.**
Amen.

WORDS OF ASSURANCE

The God who stretched out the heavens and walked the earth
    for us
is never limited to our horizons.
This God has love which passes understanding.
Receive that love. We are forgiven.
Thanks be to God!

READINGS
Proverbs 22.1–2, 8–9, 22–23
Psalm 125
James 2.1–10, 14–17
Mark 7.24–37

SERMON

PRAYER OF THANKSGIVING

We thank you that you are the one who speaks with a brave
    woman on the way,
who listens to her and does not cast aside her call for your
    generosity.
We thank you that we too can meet you on the road
and speak in freedom about our hopes and fears.
Thank you for being that sort of God in Jesus Christ.
Amen.

AFFIRMATION

In response to the word, let us affirm our faith:

**We believe that we do not own God,
we do not know all of God
and we are never God ourselves.**

**We celebrate a God
who cannot be contained
by any of our ideas,
any of our rules
or any of our plans.**

**We lift high a God
who is greater and more vulnerable than us,
who feels more than we will ever feel,
who is wiser than we will ever be,
who weeps more tears of grief than we will ever weep
and laughs in joy for our smallest moments of good,
who creates another dream each moment
and lives in freedom
beyond our widest horizons.**

PRAYER OF INTERCESSION

O God, open us to the ones who stand and face us
with their challenge for care this day.
Make their voices clear to us in the busyness of our lives,
and in our engrossment with the closer-in claims on our concern.

In this silence, give us an awareness of people
who we may not have held in compassion.

A silence is kept

These are the people who came into our hearts at this time,
   O God,
and these are the longings we have for them.

The people pray

There are others we hold before you in the silence, O God.
We pray for them too and ask that you will care for them
as you did for the woman so long ago.
We pray for ourselves too –
some prayers we may not have dared to pray before,
some we bring again, trusting in your love for us.
As the seasons circle the years,
as the sun rises and sets,
as the great stars hang low over us, your people,
night after night,
so is your faithfulness to us, O God.
And so we pray this day,
in the name of Jesus Christ.
Amen.

COMMISSIONING

Go with open lives into all the possibilities which lie before us
   in God,
our guide and our salvation.
Go with trust into an unknown path,
confident that Jesus has already walked this way before us.

BLESSING

And may springs of living water be there when we need them,
the food and wine of the feast be set before us
and resting places of peace
be the gift of the God who has come near to us.
Amen.

↫

AMONG US, EVEN US
Will new things still be found

For this service you will need

- *Pieces of coloured paper, one to be given to each person as they enter*
- *A bowl or basket on the table/altar for the receiving of the papers*

CALL TO WORSHIP

In every corner of the world:
The songs of the Creator will break forth in joy!

In the place where we have always been:
The Christ will speak new things before us.

Stay, stay here until it is time to go
as companions on the way.
In heart and mind and soul and strength, let us stay,
for here we may discover the truth in our midst.
Let us worship God!

PRAYER OF INVOCATION

Dear God, surprise us with the emerging of your spirit among us.
Open our lives to that possibility, here and now.
Come to us in ways we may never have imagined
and send us on your way with commitment and joy.
Amen.

PRAYER OF CONFESSION

As a preparation for confession,
let us think of each other in this congregation and reflect, before
    God,
on whether we always allow for new possibilities in those we
    know.

A silence is kept

Dear God,
who in Jesus was part of a homely group of people like us,
if we crush or ignore in each other the gifts which are offered:
Forgive us.

When we envy those who aspire to a new dream
or fear their challenge to us:
Forgive us.

When we load ourselves down with things which we believe that
we need
and ignore your offerings of divine resources:
Forgive us.

If we waste the economy of your mission in the world
by spending our energies on trying to insist that some respond
to us
while others wait in emptiness and hope:
Forgive us, O God.
**Forgive us and place our hands in each other's hands,
that we may live and move for you.
Amen.**

WORDS OF ASSURANCE

Christ is never defeated in us.
This, our God, is risen in hope and truth in every generation.
Travel on in lightness of heart and surrounded by grace.
Come, receive the promise of life!
**Thanks be to God!
Amen.**

READINGS

2 Samuel 5.1–5, 9–10
Psalm 48
2 Corinthians 12.2–10
Mark 6.1–13

SERMON

AFFIRMATION

In response to the word,
we affirm that there may be new possibilities among us still.
In the silence, let us write on the pieces of coloured paper in
our hands
hopes we have for new things which we have to offer,

new insights about the Gospel lying untold within our hearts
or new things we have seen in others.

The people do so

As an affirmation of faith,
let us bring these new possibilities forward and place them
on the holy table,
believing that God can take them and enhance them
for the good of all.

The people bring their papers forward and place them in the basket

PRAYER OF THANKSGIVING

Gracious God, with thankful hearts
we celebrate your eternal faithfulness to us,
your commitment to humankind,
your patience with us in all our strange and perverse ways
and your never-ending love.
There is no other God like you,
no other God who has entered our life in all its struggles and
    delights,
and who lifts up among us new voices, new prayers,
new insights and courage
and new visions for our life.
Amen.

PRAYER OF INTERCESSION

O God, in the landscape of our life together,
whether it be fertile or like the earth after drought,
we pray that you will raise up a flower of blossoming life,
or a single green leaf in the centre of our barrenness.
If the eyes of our souls see only what we expect to see,
give us new delight in the unexpected –
the flashes of colour of a hidden bird,
a sound of song in a silence
or a sound of silence in the middle of our humming life
into which the brave word falls in hope and grace.

A silence is kept and then the basket of papers is lifted high

For we would be your people of adventure and vision,
of courage and hope,
in a world of low expectation and inturned soul.
Speak through us to its lost longings, O God.
speak to us and call us on.
Help us to travel without the heavy loads of things we think
  we need,
dependent only on the resources which come from you.
In the name of the Christ,
Amen.

COMMISSIONING

Go into the world, but do not go alone.
Go with each other as loving and grace-filled companions on
  the way.
Go always with God, who is our ever-present friend and guide.

BLESSING

And may the sacred be found beside your feet,
holiness spread itself across the skies above you
and the mystery of God
break forth from every bud of life.
Amen.

꙾

FINDING WISDOM

There were once some children who were asked what sort of group they
would be prepared to join (as an entry into church membership studies).
They thought about it and then said it would be a group in which people
could be themselves; where people did not have to pretend they needed to
go to the school library at lunchtime because they did not feel part of any
group; where people who were different would not be hurt and those who
played with people who were different would still have friends; where
people would understand if people were a bit difficult and would think
maybe they had trouble at home and where there were really good
biscuits for morning tea! We hardly dared ask them if they would be
prepared to join the church. They thought the morning tea was probably
OK...

Preparation

There are places in this service where children could be involved. They will need to be prepared for their parts in the service.

CALL TO WORSHIP

God of all wisdom,
yet found in the soul of a child;
God of all that is eternal
yet glimpsed in the beauty of a fragile petal of a flower;
God of depths and heights and breadth,
God of before and beyond,
God in the great stretches of history,
yet as near to us as a humble sign of love.
Let us worship God!

PRAYER OF INVOCATION

Please, let us find you here, O God,
in all the shadowy echoes of your life,
remarkably present in ordinary people,
the old and the young, the strong and the weak.
Please, let us find you here, O God,
and give us the eyes to see each other as you have always
    found us.
Amen.

CONFESSION

Dear God, we live in a world
which mostly teaches us to find wisdom in the powerful
and in those who speak with the authority of cleverness.
We sometimes do not trust our own insights into your wisdom
and dare not test your voice within us in case others look upon us
    with scorn.
And then sometimes we trust our own wisdom
and compete for the power which we believe should be ours.

Silent reflection

O God, if we have not imagined that our children could teach
    us about you,
refusing to affirm their hopeful and sometimes confronting
    explorations towards truth

and the nature of the life of those who follow you:
Call us into a new openness, O God.

When we believe that we know most of what there is to know
and close ourselves off from the shock of newness:
Call us into a new openness, O God.

If we have stopped looking for wisdom
because we are discouraged by its small chance of survival
 among us
and fear the pain of its rejection again:
Call us into a new openness, O God,
and break through the barriers which we raise in so many ways.
Amen.

WORDS OF ASSURANCE

God is never defeated by our failings.
The wisdom of God will arise again in us and in every generation.
This is the testimony of history.
This is the witness of faith to us in Holy Scripture.
All those who come this day in faith will be given the gifts of new
 possibilities.
Thanks be to God!

READINGS

Proverbs 31.10–31
Psalm 1
James 3.13—4.3, 7–8a
Mark 9.30–37

SERMON

Or:

Thoughts from children about how they would like to change the world
or the church

PRAYER OF THANKSGIVING

Thank you God, that you are not confined by our lack of wonder.
Thank you God, that you are never defined by the limits of our
 small expectations.

Thank you God, that you act outside all of our preconceived ideas.
And thank you God, that as we see you in a little child, so we may
   honour the child within ourselves.
Amen.

PRAYER OF INTERCESSION
This prayer could be replaced by one from a child or several children

God of grace and all wisdom,
we live in a world which often seems so complex and ambiguous
that we cannot find ways through to act with courage and clarity.
Breathe your holy wisdom into this time, O God.

We often find ideas and authorities swirling around us
in many voices which say they hold the truth
and it is hard to know who to trust.
Breathe your holy wisdom into this place, O God.

Sometimes our life in the church is filled with too many options,
too many calls for our action and time, too many cries of need.
Breathe your holy wisdom into your church, O God.

Sometimes we hardly pause to wait for your wisdom in our own
   lives, O God,
as we race through the days or follow our own determined path.
**Stop us in our tracks and breathe your holy wisdom into us,
   O God.**

A silence is kept

The whole universe speaks of your wisdom, O God,
in every marvellous pattern of existence,
in all the harmonies and interplay of all that is.
Even as we can never fully understand it, we marvel at its
   wonders
and the even greater mystery that you would bend to speak in us.
Be with us, O God of all wisdom.
Amen.

COMMISSIONING
Go in faith to search for the wisdom of God.
Go to find it in unexpected places and to lift it up in hope.
Go, because we might well find it in the heart of a child.

BLESSING

And may a little child take you by the hand and lead you to the
    feet of God,
the child of Bethlehem lift your eyes to the star for your guiding
and the childlike joy of the Spirit dance before you.
Amen.

◞

FROM THE HEART

For this service you will need

- *It would be good to have at the centre symbols of vulnerability, like
  small soft birds gathered at the foot of a cross, fragile flowers in a bowl,
  or very tiny candles*

CALL TO WORSHIP

The heart of God, how could we name it?
In songs of praise, in psalms of joy, in stories of grace,
in waving forest and bushland,
and flowers beside the road,
in a hand stretched out on a city street
and everlasting sweeps of mountain grandeur.
The heart of God, how could we name it?
In the tender softness of the face of a new child
and the wrinkles of life on the hand of the old,
in a hidden kindness of a homely neighbour
and the public costly love of the martyrs for the people.
In the heart of God lies all good and truth.
The heart of God is beyond our naming.
Let us worship God.

PRAYER OF INVOCATION

Be found within our hearts today, O God.
Be seen there in all that we do and all that we are for each other
    this day.
Come and stay with us, deep within the inner life of each one
and carried forth into the world which always waits for your
    coming.
Amen.

CONFESSION

Dear God, sometimes we even fool ourselves.
We confess that sometimes we tell ourselves that we are engaged
    in your life
when our actions have become an empty shell of habit and form:
Forgive us, O God.

We may have looked upon others in judgement,
because they do not do as we do,
and have failed to see their inner integrity:
Forgive us, O God.

Sometimes we are harsh with ourselves,
condemning our own faltering journey
towards honest and authentic relationship with you
when you do not condemn us at all:
Forgive us and heal us, O God.

And sometimes we stand alongside those who have become the
    people of the law,
rather than the people of your loving heart and spirit
and fail to see what is important and what is not:
Forgive our lack of courage and poverty of spirit, O God.
Amen.

WORDS OF ASSURANCE

The God we love looks on the heart
and sees the truth of our longing for forgiveness,
the struggle of our varying journeys
and all the complexities of our life.
Trust this God, the God of grace.
We are forgiven!
Amen.

READINGS

Song of Songs 2.8–13
Psalm 45.1–2, 6–9
James 1.17–27
Mark 7.1–8, 14–15, 21–23

SERMON

PRAYER OF THANKSGIVING

O God, we are thankful that you do not see us as others see us,
or sometimes even as we see ourselves.
So often we are less loving than you are and our judgements are
    harsh and wounding.
We come to you with grateful hearts and celebrate that because
    you are God,
you are more than we can ever be.
Amen.

PRAYER OF INTERCESSION

There are moments, O God,
when we long to reach out and touch the world with your love,
when our souls burn with the fire of your passion for your whole
    creation.
We look upon the people and name them as made in your image,
due for honour and deep respect as they struggle on
in the toil and rewards of human life.

Silent reflection

In faith we pray for them today.
Because you have been faithful to us,
we know that you will be present with them too.
These are the ones who are closest to our concern on this day.

The people name those for whom they are concerned

Take each one in your hand today, O God,
and do not let them fall.
Care for them as you do each small sparrow and each lily of the
    field,
cherishing them on their way and watching over them.

The symbols of vulnerability are lifted up or small candles lit

Come close to us too, O God.
Come into our hearts and search out our deepest unsaid prayers,
for sometimes we dare not even ask for what we need,
or we do not know what it is that will help us.

Be present with us this day, O God.
In the name of the Christ,
Amen.

COMMISSIONING

Follow your hearts into the paths of mercy,
for so is the heart of God.
Follow your souls into the ways of truth,
truth revealed within the heart of the Spirit of God.
Go in faith.

BLESSING

And may the places where you walk become sacred spaces of the
   Holy God,
the places where you take your stand be signposts to the love of
   Christ,
the places where you rest be filled with the renewing grace of the
   Spirit.
Amen.

In This Hour, We Prepare for the Next Challenge

May truth be a belt around our waist,
righteousness be our breastplate,
our shoes carry us into the paths of peace
and the salvation of God always cover our heads.

ADD TO OUR LIFE

For this service you will need

- *The table could be dressed with a swirling blue cloth coming from a cross and a basket of loaves and fishes*

CALL TO WORSHIP

Greater than all we have in our human hands:
God of plenty and gifts.

Greater than all the storms and swirling powers which threaten
    to destroy us:
God of risen life.

Greater than we are, even in our best moments,
even in our largest loving,
even in the deepest dreams and visions of our hearts:
You are our God, the God of all eternity.
Let us worship our God!

INVOCATION

Come, gracious Jesus, even though we are rarely ready
for the surprising ways in which your presence is made known
    to us.
Come, gracious Jesus, and remind us of your generous life
and our capacity to share with you in the feeding of the world.
Come, gracious Jesus, as we gather around to meet you, as did
    your first disciples.
Amen.

CONFESSION

Great God of the universe,
we confess that sometimes we act as though you are not God.

Silent reflection

When we live our life
as though we do not need you;
if we fail to notice you walking on water beside us
as we struggle with our fear;

when we leave the world with its problems and longings
as though the resources of your power are of no use;
and if we do not offer you what we have
because we believe it has little significance in your plan:
Forgive us, O God.
Challenge us with the mystery of your grace
and call us into your company.
Amen.

ASSURANCE

Look, the hands of Jesus wait for our gifts!
Look, Christ Jesus comes to us across the waters of life!
Do not be afraid.
This is the word to us today and every day.
Live with faith, forgiveness is ours.
Thanks be to God!

READINGS

2 Samuel 11.1–13
Psalm 14
Ephesians 3.14–21
John 6.1–21

SERMON

AFFIRMATION OF FAITH

Let us affirm our faith:

We believe that what we see before us is never all that is
    possible,
that beyond our present is a future which could be new
with more than enough for all,
and compassion greater than our own.

We believe in a God
who comes to the fearful people
across waters of life which threaten to swamp us
and whose company is love
beyond our understanding.

We believe in a greater power for good
than anything within each of us and all of us,

which stands between us
and at the centre of the universe
in ways of mystery and grace.

PRAYER OF INTERCESSION

Dear God, often we say of ourselves,
'Who are we among so many people who need your love and
    care?'
We feel so few, so weak, as we stand before your mission in the
    world.
We can't imagine what to do and sometimes what to pray
in response to the complex issues, the dimensions of the need,
the forces which confront us
as we listen to the voices of those who cry out.

The people name the voices they hear

Pray for us, Holy Spirit,
and give to us new understandings for our task.
Give to us a sense of your power
to walk towards us across the rough waters,
unimpeded by our lack of faith,
undeterred by our anxious souls
and uncluttered by our confusions and small of hopes.
For you are the great God of all time,
of all people and in every place.
and we pray in your name,
Amen.

COMMISSIONING

We are always near to the land of the power of God.
Hold hard to the Christ,
who is beside us in the boat
and take up your calling as the disciples of Christ.

BLESSING

And may you be embraced by the arms of the loving parent,
taken firmly by the hand of Jesus our Saviour
and covered by the warming wings of the Spirit.
Amen.

PUT ON THE ARMOUR OF GOD

For this service you will need

- *A large candle*
- *A number of small candles and tapers*
- *A large Bible*

CALL TO WORSHIP

The armour of God is strong and gentle,
arising from the Spirit within us:
The Spirit is our strength.

The mantle of God is warm and filled with light,
the transparency of those who lived covered with faith alone:
Christ is our courage.

The candle is lit

The breastplate of God is a hollow hand of sanctuary,
firmly held around us as a mother's love and a father's grace:
The Creator is our beginning and our ending.
Let us worship God!

PRAYER OF INVOCATION

We are gathered here together, O God of all generations,
waiting in hope for the strength to be your people.
Come among us in passionate life
that we may be more truly those who are given to you for your
    mission in the world.
In our frailty, breathe into us the power of your Spirit today.
Amen.

CONFESSION

God, who is like a rock before the great forces of destruction,
clad only in a deathly cross and bleeding side,
we confess that the life which we choose to live with you
often hardly needs any armour at all.

Silent reflection

Sometimes, O God, when we do arm ourselves
it is only for our own defence,
our own ideas,
our own power and pride,
our own place in the approval of others.
Forgive us, O God.

Sometimes we use your armour,
our respected place in your church,
to cover who we are or who we are not,
to add to our own self-righteousness,
rather than your task
of costly love for others.
Forgive us, O God.

Sometimes we believe that we must be defended
in ways which you would never have used
and then we remember your loving kindness,
and the sword laid down when it might have defended you.
Forgive us when we betray you, O Jesus Christ.
Forgive us and call us again.
Amen.

WORDS OF ASSURANCE

Jesus loves us, even to the death.
The voice of God is as the dove in its comfort and hope.
Take on the renewal of the Holy Spirit,
for where the Spirit of Christ is, there is liberty.
This is for us, even us.
Thanks be to God!
Amen.

READINGS

1 Kings 8.1, 6, 10–11
Psalm 84
Ephesians 6.10–20
John 6.56–69

SERMON

AFFIRMATION OF FAITH

In response to the word, let us affirm our faith:

**In the toughness and traumas of life,
we are never left defenceless,
for the covering of God
lies around us stronger than any deaths.**

**We believe in a God who showed us
with open arms stretched out on a killing cross
the power of good to defend the faithful,
to rise free in strong life again
in an eternal challenge
to all the forces that would destroy us.**

**In our every day,
we believe that we are given energies for survival,
cherishing and healing,
courage and renewal
to face all that stands between us
and the victory of love.**

PRAYER OF INTERCESSION

God of all history, God of our history,
direct us to your vision for this day and our place.
Inspire us to catch the majesty of your dreams
so that we will dare not move towards them without carrying
     with us
the mystery of your life within us and around us.
Inspire us with the wonder of the breadth of all that you imagine
so that we will long with all our heart and mind and strength to be
     part of it.

We will light small candles now as we name the possibilities
which we see, the flickering hopes which may be fanned by
     faithfulness.

The people do so

Around these frail flames of hope,
we place the armour of your word to us, O God.

The Bible is placed behind the candle

We are as nothing without your care for us, O God.
We stand naked and trembling unless you cloak us
in the rigour of your determination to bring in a new heaven and
  a new earth.
Stand with us,
come with us,
give us a lightness of heart, O God.
Give us joy along the way,
persistence and creativity
and bright dreams of things beyond our sight.
Amen.

COMMISSIONING

Take it on now, the clothing of the life of Christ!
Our calling sounds as a trumpet,
in the cries of the people and the groaning of the creation.
Let us not stay any longer on this holy hill,
but go in the name of Christ.

BLESSING

And may truth be a belt around our waist,
righteousness be our breastplate,
our shoes carry us into the paths of peace
and the salvation of God always cover our heads.
Amen.

⟿

THE BREAD OF ETERNAL LIFE

For this service you will need

- *Baskets of bread, enough to share around the congregation, placed on the table or altar alongside a cross*

CALL TO WORSHIP

There is a God who calls us on,
spreading life into all the universe,
like the veins in the leaves of a tree.
Let us worship this God.

There is a God who grows faith from emptiness,
and great dreams from shadows of doubt,
for whom the desert is the foundation of nurturing love.
Let us worship this God.

There is a God who will not invite in us false life,
which rests on fruitless dependencies,
and shallow associations.
Let us worship this God.
Let us live and grow to wholeness.

INVOCATION

God, who never rests until we live in fullness,
come to us, not as soft and painless things which lie easily in our
    midst
and seduce us into wanting more and more.
Be with us in the rigour of our life and the rigour of your
    loving,
your presence inviting us into maturity of life and faith.
Amen.

CONFESSION

Dear God, we would often rather not grow up.
It feels safe and comfortable to be fed by you
and to come back for more before we have lived from your
    feeding.
It is sometimes even attractive to us
to present your word like that to others,
selling them short as we protect them
from the truth of your costly life.
Forgive us, Jesus who is the Bread.

If we have failed to see the difference
between your gifts of rest and recreation
and easy ways of walking through life:
Forgive us, Jesus who is the Way.

When we ignore the calling which lies in the gifts which are ours
and let them wither away from lack of use:
Forgive us, Jesus who is the Truth.

If we choose half-life,
rather than the passion of all that you call us to be:
Forgive us, Jesus Christ who is the life in all creation.
Amen.

WORDS OF ASSURANCE

In Jesus Christ, we are always called forth again into newness.
The bread of life is ours for the eating this day.
The way is stretched out before us for our choosing.
The promise of God is that we are never offered less than this.
Thanks be to God!

PRAYER OF THANKSGIVING

Let us sing a song of thanksgiving to our God!
God, you hover over our life like the beauty of the northern and
    southern stars,
and flow through our existence like the rivers of the earth.
You breathe among us like the gentle winds
and stand firm under our feet like the rock of ages.
We thank you that we are never alone.
Amen.

READINGS
2 Samuel 11.26—12.13a
Psalm 51.1–12
Ephesians 4.1–16
John 6.24–35

SERMON

PRAYER OF INTERCESSION

Dear God, you call us into self-respecting life.
Strengthen our will to lift up our heads and live.
Sharpen our determination to look around us for the task you give
    to us.

Silent reflection

Sometimes we are puzzled about how best to show our love for
    others, O God.
Sometimes we like being needed too much.

Sometimes we find it hard to tell the difference
between our love running out and the need for others to be
    self-reliant.
Give to us a love like yours which is faithful and true.
Give to us the wisdom to see the difference
between caring for others and drawing life away from them.

Silent reflection

Dear God, we bring before you your church in all its humanness.
We know that, even as you call us to claim eternal life,
you never break the bruised reed in us or in anyone.
Your very love for us creates a new and safer place for growing
    stronger.
May we also offer that to others.
These are the ones who need that cherishing place now, O God.

The people bring their prayers for others

Feed these people with the bread of your life, O God.
Place the bread of life in our hands to take into the world.

The bread is passed around the people

O God, may this bread become in us bread for the world.
**Look upon the world with your eyes of loving concern
and spread a table before us all which is like a feast.
Look upon us with eyes that see into our hearts and souls
and sustain us for a greater good.
In your name we pray in faith,
Amen.**

COMMISSIONING

Stand tall as the people of God,
take the bread of life in your hands and go into the world
in courage and strength.
Stand tall and look for a new adventure of faith.
It waits for us now as the children of God.

BLESSING
And may Christ Jesus look into your face with love,
God the Creator spring to life within your being
and the Holy Spirit be found in sacred spaces around you.
Amen.

⤳

WALK IN THE FOOTSTEPS

*This service could be used for a time of confirmation, of anniversary. It is
for a time of 'tribal' bonding and encouragement.*

For this service you will need

- *A sand pathway: sand sprinkled on a long strip of heavy plastic spread
  down through the centre aisle or across the front of the church*
- *A wooden or metal cross which can be pressed into the sand to make a
  cross shape, and another cross with a stand*

OPENING
We walk in the footsteps of those who have gone before
and know that we are not alone on this journey.
We walk in the footsteps of those who are older
and know that they go before us.
We walk in the footsteps of God
for the feet of our God have walked this way.
**The footsteps of God will become for us
the Way, the Truth and the Life.
Thanks be to God!**

CONFESSION
You did walk among us, Jesus Christ,
and we turned your footsteps into the mark of the cross.

*A cross is pressed into the sand and a standing cross is placed at the end
of the sand pathway*

Still we often require your Godliness among us to take that shape,
the shape of costliness.

Silent reflection

In our history we have tried to kill the good.
We remember the martyrs, the ones who have suffered
in the cause of love and justice.

Names are said and the cross shape is marked at intervals in the sand

We tread our life behind these marks of the cross, O God.
In them lie our pain, our shame,
but also our respect for faithfulness and our joy that good is never
    finally defeated.
Forgive us when we leave the path of truth, O God,
when we follow our own lesser paths
and lose the way.
Forgive us, O God and call us back.
Amen.

WORDS OF ASSURANCE

The cross stands before us as a sign of the costly love of God.
Receive that love, even as we have lost our way.
Turn around and see the footsteps of Christ, the way to life.
This is a free gift to us all.
Amen.

READINGS

SERMON

AFFIRMATION OF FAITH

Let us affirm our faith together:

The footsteps of God
are there for us,
marked in the creation
in countless gifts and beauties.
They lie there before us
in patterns of harmony and interweaving,
in survivals against the odds
and brave bright life.

The footsteps of God
are there for us

in the light tread of the Christ,
leaving hollows of love and grace,
inviting us to put our feet within God's life
and find ourselves deep in meaning,
held into purpose
and carried forward into fullness.

The footsteps of God
are there for us
in the mystery of the Spirit,
gently touching the earth with comfort,
leaving tracks of truth and courage,
and lifting her feet
in dancings of delight
which leap over our laws,
our limits,
our boundaries on love.

PRAYER OF INTERCESSION

We thank you, O God,
for all those whose footsteps lead us on towards you
and your way to life.
We remember all those among us and in the world
who are beginning on their paths in life.
We remember our children and young people today.

Their names are said

Keep them safe, O God,
and carry them into a great adventure of life and faith,
one which calls forth in them all that they are and could be.
Then set them down in a peaceful place, O God,
that they may find rest and play and the joys of being human.
We remember also all children around the world,
who may be in places and situations
where we who have gone before have led them into risk
and suffering,
those who are hungry, homeless,
working too hard for their tender years,
caught in war and fear.

The people and places are named

O God, hear our prayer.
O God, make clear footsteps for us to follow you,
that there may be less pain and more justice
in all the world
and your creation left whole and healthy
for their inheritance.
We ask these things in the name of Christ,
Amen.

SENDING OUT

Let us leave our unique footsteps in the sand.
What is in your footsteps for those who follow?
In the silence, reflect on one thing that you wish to leave there.

A silence is kept

When you are ready, go and make a footstep in the sand
and, if you wish, share with your neighbour
what you would like to leave for those who follow.

The people make their footsteps and share

Come, let us leave this place together!
Go in faith into the world to make footsteps which lead to life.

BLESSING

And may the Creator guide us on,
Christ Jesus take our hand if we falter
and the Spirit call us on with sweet singing.
Amen.

GATHERING TOGETHER

For this service you will need

- *A long tape or wide ribbon which will be placed around the edge of the church, circling the congregation*
- *Coloured plain sticker labels, with backing still intact, given one to each person as they enter*
- *Baskets of pens*

CALL TO WORSHIP

As the sea gathers its waters for the next waves on the shore:
So God gathers the people for loving.

As the notes of harmony congregate for the sound of music:
So God places us in clusterings of community.

As the wind sweeps the air into great clouds of beauty:
So God sees the wonder of our unity in all creation.

Let us worship this God!

PRAYER OF INVOCATION

Dear God, your persistence in building the relationships
between us and with you,
your holding together in peace and love
of all things that you have created
encourages us to invite the revealing of your Spirit here with us
    today.
Come and show us who we might be together
and who else we might invite into your presence with us.
Amen.

PRAYER OF CONFESSION

Gathering God, our vision for community is never as loving as
    yours.
We confess that there are people who we would rather not bring
    near to us or to you.

Silent reflection

Forgive us when our love is not like your love.
If we really think others are not worthy to approach you
and that we are more worthy than they are:
**Forgive us, O God, and remind us that none of us is worthy,
that your love is a free gift to all of us.**

When we demand that people achieve our measure of good
or our perceptions of the right way to be with you:
**Forgive us, O God, and remind us that we are not God
and that there are many paths towards you.**

If we think we can put boundaries around your love
and hold you to ourselves within our own community of faith:
**Forgive us, O God, and remind us that we will never own you
and that you break free of all our limitations.**

We confess, before the bounty of your life,
that we often make you a small God in our own image.
**Forgive us, yet again, O God of Grace.
Amen.**

WORDS OF ASSURANCE

The forgiveness of God surpasses all that we can ever know.
Even as God gathers the world into costly grace,
so we are included, and we are no longer strangers.
Take your place in the love of God!
Amen!

READINGS

2 Samuel 7.1–14a
Psalm 89.20–37
Ephesians 2.11–22
Mark 6.30–34, 53–56

SERMON

AFFIRMATION

We are gathered together by God.

The ribbon is carried and placed around the people

Let us affirm the power of God to gather more things together
than we have here:
different sorts of people,
parts of the creation that need our care,
things in our own lives which need acceptance and more care or
    forgiveness,
groups of people or situations which need our compassionate
    prayer and action.

I invite you now to write some of those things on the stickers
which you received when you came in and stick them on to the
ribbon which is on the edges of our life here today as a sign that
we would like to gather them in among us.

The people do so

PRAYER OF INTERCESSION
God of community,
Enlarge our community, gathering in these people and concerns
we see as lying on the edges of our life.
As we look at our world fraught with wars, sometimes religious
    wars,
we know that we need the same power that people of old saw in
    Jesus Christ.
Send to us this power for peace and healing, O God.

Send us Christ's power for seeing the truth in each situation,
for pointing to the forces which destroy
and to those activities which will bring people together again.
Send to us this power for peace and healing, O God.

Remind us of the costly journey towards your reign
so that we will not be satisfied with casual solutions
and go on searching for quick and easy ways.
Send to us this power for peace and healing, O God.

Give to us, too, a sense of your loving kindness towards us,
a faith in your permission to rest and draw apart
so that we may be made new and see things more clearly
in the quiet of your company.

Send to us this power for peace and healing,
for gathering in community, O God,
for you are our only hope,
you are the one who never sees us as strangers,
for you have met us in Jesus Christ.
Amen.

COMMISSIONING

Go into the world to meet the people.
Go into the world to find them no longer strangers,
but the loved children of God,
waiting for the other children of God to emerge.

BLESSING

And may the face of Christ be seen in those you meet,
the love of the Creator shine in all creation as we look
and the warmth of the Spirit radiate in every place.
Amen.

⌐⌐

ACCEPTING THE MANTLE OF LEADERSHIP
For those being asked to accept the responsibility of a
particular leadership

For this ritual you will need

- *A coloured cloth to be used as a 'mantle' – could be a scarf or a shawl*
- *Lengths of knotted gold thread each with a safety pin attached*
- *A small candle*
- *A large candle*
- *Wine or another form of celebratory drink for all present*

WEARING THE MANTLE

The mantle of leadership is like a cloak.
It announces the colouring of our life, it covers us on the way
and it weighs upon our shoulders as we walk.

The mantle is placed upon the table

There is both preparation and recognition in this moment
for the formal receiving of the mantle of leadership.
There is a calling and the offering of the company of God.

THE GIFTS

There are many different gifts to be received in this community of
  people
and we have already discovered them among us:
gifts which are for us all and gifts which are within each one,
gifts of the Holy Spirit.
I invite you to remember the gifts which you have seen and
  received
and to pin a golden thread upon the mantle as you name it.

The people name the gifts which they have seen

ENDING AND BEGINNING
As we approach the hour of inviting leadership in one of us,
as we walk on wearing the golden threads of giftedness which are
  ours,
maybe we have found in this experience of reflection, community
  and learning
new ways of being people together in friendship and networking.

*The people may like to share about this and add more golden threads to
the mantle*

THANKSGIVING
Thanks be to God for all that we have received
as we approach this significant hour in our life together.
Thanks be to God for wisdom and inspiration,
for hope and faith.
Thanks be to God!

A GRIEVING
With each other,
we have seen new possibilities for the transformation of the world
and new possibilities for receiving leadership in this.
As we look into our own future,
if we are fearful of what lies before us,

if we find the price of leadership and giftedness too high
or if the forces standing in our way seem too great,
let us grieve together and honour our fragile humanness.
Let us place this small candle beside the mantle,
the delicate, flickering light of our resolve.

A small candle is lit and placed and a silence is kept

Do not be afraid.
**The victory is already won in Jesus Christ
and we are never left alone.**

ASSUMING THE MANTLE
In spite of our human weakness,
some of us are called to leadership,
leadership which involves courage
and the accepting of responsibility in faith.

The person/people come forward

We invite you to take this mantle, place it upon your shoulders,
wear it like a mantle of hope
and share any new possibility
which you have seen for yourself as a leader.

The person/people share their hopes

And now we remember the leadership of the world.

A large candle is lit

Let us share any hopes which we have
for the transformation of the community around us and the wider
    world
into a place of justice, love, peace, creativity and freedom.

The people share

Nothing is impossible. Nothing is inevitable.
In the face of all that confronts us,
in the face of our own fears and human limitations,
we are still the people of courage and freedom,
of vision and responsibility.

Let us go into another day,
carrying around us the stories of hope,
faith in a new dream
and the power of a loving God.
The world waits for people who will carry it forward into a new
    day.
It waits for us.

People are offered glasses of wine

Let us raise our glasses to this new day and our part in it!

WALK IN LOVE

For this service you will need

• *A warm red woollen cloth*

CALL TO WORSHIP

Walk in love!
It is stretched out like the heavens above us.
It is laid like a carpet of earth beneath our feet.
It surrounds us like the bright rays of the sun
and the sweet sounds of the gently falling rain.
Walk in love!
Love is like this warm covering around our shoulders.

A warm red woollen cloth is lifted high and placed on the table

It is to be trusted forever.
It threads through all generations,
red with the bleeding of its costliness.
Its raw rigour speaks of things which we dare not name,
in the reality of our struggling life,
honoured and graced by God.
Let us worship God!

PRAYER OF INVOCATION

It is through you that we come to God, Jesus Christ.
You, who were with the Creator from the beginning,

making a pathway to God in every time and every place
and revealed to us more clearly as you walked our way in
     Palestine.
Come to us today in ways which we can understand again,
O God of loving-kindness.
Amen.

CONFESSION

We confess before you that we do not always live
as those who walk in your love, O God of grace.
We sometimes live as those who walk with a harsh and punishing
     God,
one who looks nothing like you, Jesus Christ.

Silent reflection

If we have lived with a God of our own making,
smaller and meaner than you would ever be:
Forgive us, O God, and expand your loving life in us.

If we refuse your forgiveness
because we cannot imagine loving ourselves:
Forgive us, O God, and expand your loving life in us.

If we separate others from your love
by our lack of grace and compassion:
Forgive us, O God, and expand your loving life in us.

When we doubt your love
because others stand between us and your love for us:
Forgive us, and expand your loving life in us,
you who came to us in truth in Jesus Christ.
Amen.

WORDS OF ASSURANCE

Receive the forgiveness of God and walk again in love.
This is an act of faith,
an act which will carry us into grace upon grace.
Let us be the people of faith and believe that
we are forgiven!
Thanks be to God.

READINGS

2 Samuel 18.5–9
Psalm 130
Ephesians 4.25—5.2
John 6.35, 41–51

SERMON

PRAYER OF INTERCESSION

Dear God, as we look at the world,
we see so many people gasping for love,
dying because of lack of love,
and longing for signs of love.
We see people killing each other
in ways which brutalize the whole of humanity.
We watch pointless acts of destruction that achieve nothing
except brutal moments of power over others.
We see thousands of people struggling in cold and homelessness,
in hunger and fear, because we will not pay the price of loving
    each other,
in the long struggle for peace and an end to oppression.
We watch our efforts to bring love sometimes with bombs and
    terror,
to enforce the reign of love by force.

Silent reflection

Around us, we see the most vulnerable and abused people
crushed by those among us who have never known
what it means to have a little love around,
or needs beyond those they have experienced themselves.
**Give to us hearts of compassion, souls of care
and the commitment to love beyond the commonplace, O God.
Give to us love made flesh that all may walk in that love.
Amen.**

COMMISSIONING

Walk in love and carry that love around you like a warm covering
wherever you may go.

*The people pass the warm cloth to each other, placing it around each
other's shoulders*

Walk in love into a harsh world
and transform tomorrow.
This is our commission as the people of God.

BLESSING

And may our future rest with the God of eternity,
the hours be lived with Jesus Christ
and the moments be carried onwards in the life of the Spirit.
Amen.

Index of Themes